RISK TERRAIN MODELING

RISK TERRAIN MODELING

Crime Prediction and Risk Reduction

Joel M. Caplan
Leslie W. Kennedy

 UNIVERSITY OF CALIFORNIA PRESS

University of California Press, one of the most distinguished university presses in the United States, enriches lives around the world by advancing scholarship in the humanities, social sciences, and natural sciences. Its activities are supported by the UC Press Foundation and by philanthropic contributions from individuals and institutions. For more information, visit www.ucpress.edu.

University of California Press
Oakland, California

Library of Congress Cataloging-in-Publication Data

Names: Caplan, Joel M., 1980- author. | Kennedy, Leslie W., author.
   Title: Risk terrain modeling : crime prediction and risk reduction / Joel M. Caplan and Leslie W. Kennedy.
   Description: Oakland, California : University of California Press, [2016] | "2016 | Includes bibliographical references and index.
   Identifiers: LCCN 2015041323 (print) | LCCN 2015042885 (ebook) | ISBN 9780520282933 (pbk. : alk. paper) | ISBN 9780520958807 (ebook)
   Subjects: LCSH: Crime analysis—Statistical methods. | Spatial analysis (Statistics) | Crime—Environmental aspects. | Crime forecasting—Geographic information systems. | Crime prevention.
   Classification: LCC HV7936.C88 C36 2016 (print) | LCC HV7936.C88 (ebook) | DDC 364.01/422—dc23
   LC record available at http://lccn.loc.gov/2015041323

Printed in China

25 24 23 22 21 20 19 18 17 16
10 9 8 7 6 5 4 3 2 1

The paper used in this publication meets the minimum requirements of ANSI/NISO Z39.48–1992 (R 2002) (*Permanence of Paper*).

CONTENTS

LIST OF FIGURES

LIST OF TABLES

PREFACE

Criminologists have long sought to explain why crime occurs at certain places and times. These inquiries have led to a wide-ranging research literature that documents many different factors that contribute to the spatial and temporal dynamics of illegal behavior and crime victimization. There has been extensive work documenting the motivations and actions of people who commit crime, which has focused over a long period of time on victims and the conditions under which they become targets of crime, as well as the effects that this experience has on them. Criminologists have considered victims and offenders in context, examining how where they live, where they work, and where they find entertainment increase the likelihood of crime occurring. What form this context are the activities that individuals pursue as well as the nature of the environments they occupy. Some places, we know, are more likely to be locations of crime than others, that is, they are places where exposure to crime events is relatively high. This may be because of the characteristics of people who frequent these places, or because of the qualities of the environments themselves. If we concentrate on the characteristics of people, we can focus on their propensity to offend or, for victims, their susceptibility to offending. If we concentrate on the characteristics of places, we can focus on the factors that are conducive to crime occurrence, offering a means for targeting certain places that are more likely to promote illegal behavior. Both approaches have merit and have helped researchers create a more complete picture of the underlying processes that contribute to crime. The task of the criminologist is not simply to explain what is happening but also to provide prescriptions for how to use knowledge to combat crime and its consequences.

This call for actionable knowledge to inform strategies in crime reduction has long been a part of the discipline. In recent years, even more attention has been placed on making criminology practically relevant. There is a great deal of disagreement about how this should be done, however (see Lum, 2009). Notwithstanding, the call for a "translational criminology," taking research and putting it into practice, has challenged researchers to consider their work in light of its implications for informed decision making and actions in deterring and preventing crime. This call has been particularly loud in the area of policing, where evidence-based practices have grown. The data traditionally employed are used to monitor police practices, but there is an increased demand for information to assist in predicting where crime will occur and to preemptively mitigate spatial and situational risks. There have been new attempts at targeting high-risk offenders and their networks, as well as at identifying victims and working with them to reduce their reexposure to crime. This has led to programs that track repeat offenders and their network of friends and acquaintances (see Braga & Weisburd, 2012). But police are not only interested in who the offenders are; they are interested in where crimes occur. Identifying high-risk offenders controls some crime well, but chronic criminogenic places, where offending may be a consequence of ongoing interactions and opportunities, pose serious challenges to police agencies.

Police have used data-monitoring procedures to track where crime occurs and to put more resources into "hot spots." If crime occurs frequently in these areas, the reasoning goes, the police need to go there and stop it. Interestingly enough, though, the same areas appear as hot spots over long periods of time, raising the issue of why policing there has not been effective in cooling the hot spots down. Is it the case that there is something going on at these locations that continues to support illegal activity? What makes offenders prefer these locations time and again? What can we learn from the things that criminologists have already discovered about the social and physical contexts of crime that would help address this problem? If we can identify the factors that attract illegal behavior, can we use this information to forecast where crime will occur in the future? In answering these questions, we can consider existing knowledge about offenders and hot spots (that is, exposures) in the context of environmental risk (that is, vulnerability).

The concepts of vulnerability and exposure set the framework for this book. Our strategy is translational: we offer the underlying theoretical and empirical bases for the study of these concepts and then show how they can be put into practical use in studying the spatial dynamics of crime. People can live in vulnerable areas (defined by an agreed-upon set of criminogenic features), but in the absence of motivated offenders, the risk of crime is relatively low. So, the risk of crime is a function of spatial vulnerability within the context of other factors that carry different weights relative to one another in influencing outcomes. Crime risks are both place-based and situational, that is, they are affected both by exposure to individual events that appear from location to location and by exposure to places where events are known to cluster over time. The concept of exposure defines risk as a spatial-temporal function of previous crime events. Cartographically modeling vulnerability as the clustering of environmental risk factors and their spatial influences and then interpreting vulnerability in the context of exposure promote a strategy to identify, monitor, and manage these settings. This approach matches the work on environmental risk assessment that makes a distinction between the vulnerability that emerges from conditions that are conducive to the appearance of certain types of problems (for example, health hazards, disasters, or public security events) and the characteristics of events or individuals that enhance their exposure to these hazards (Van Brunschot & Kennedy, 2008).

Our approach to studying the spatial dynamics of crime is based on the ability to take account of many different factors in a comprehensive assessment that can be adapted across crime types and locations. This approach is possible because of the development of advanced mapping technologies and sophisticated analytical approaches for interpreting place-based risk. In addition, data collection has improved for both crime outcomes and environmental features that can be included in the spatial modeling. We use raster-based mapping techniques, which provide a comprehensive approach to crime analysis and standardize risk factors into common geographic units. Separate map layers representing the presence, absence, spatial influence, and intensity of each risk factor at every place throughout a landscape are created with a geographic information system (GIS) and then all risk map layers are combined to produce a composite "risk terrain" map with attribute values that account for the compounded risk at every place throughout the landscape. Rigorous research studies, discussed in this book, have demonstrated how theoretically and empirically grounded risk terrain maps can articulate places where conditions are suitable and most likely for crimes to occur.

The resulting approach, risk terrain modeling (RTM), fits well into contemporary police practices by articulating officers' gut feelings and their perceptions of the risk of places beyond merely referencing past occurrences of reported crimes or hot spots. RTM methods provide police with a common language and means to communicate criminogenic risk and to work proactively to protect against features of the landscape that attract or enable crime. This has led to new approaches to police productivity that reduce the heavy reliance on traditional law enforcement actions, such as stops, arrests, and citations. As an analytical method, RTM articulates a landscape of place-based risks and identifies and helps prioritize evidence-based responses to mitigate risks. This encourages a focus on places, not just on people located at certain places, which could jeopardize public perceptions of police and negatively affect community relations. With the growing utilization of intelligence-led operations in the law enforcement community, studying the spatial dynamics of crime with RTM is especially important for tactical actions, resource allocations, and short- and long-term strategic planning.

In RTM, "risk" refers to the probability of an occurrence of an undesired outcome (for example, crime), determined by the increased spatial vulnerability at places. "Terrain" refers to a study extent of equally sized grid cells whose attributes quantify vulnerabilities at each place (that is, cell). And "modeling" refers to attributing the presence, absence, influence, or intensity of qualities of the real world to places within a terrain in order to study their simultaneous effect on the risk of undesired outcomes.

RTM is for all intents and purposes a diagnostic method. With a diagnosis of the attractors of criminal behavior, we can make very accurate forecasts of where crime will occur. RTM considers the factors that are conducive to crime, including an acknowledgment that different crime types may have different correlates that increase the risk of their occurrence. It provides a way in which the combined factors that contribute to criminal behavior can be targeted, connections to crime can be monitored, spatial vulnerabilities can be assessed, and actions can be taken to reduce the worst effects.

As we formulated RTM, we realized that we needed to develop a clear understanding of what factors relate to the risk of certain crime outcomes and how to make these findings actionable. We wanted our approach to be based on research, assuming that we could learn a great deal from the established results of research that had been done on various crime types. Over many decades, researchers have expended considerable effort in identifying links between certain factors and specific crime outcomes. RTM provides the framework to synthesize these insights by linking them to geography, which is their common denominator, thereby applying all of these empirical findings to practice simultaneously. But RTM does not rely only on past research findings. As we discuss in this book, the experiences and insights of police, crime analysts, and other practitioners are just as important for creating meaningful risk assessments.

This book shows the technical steps and practical applications of RTM through the presentation of empirical research and case studies. We intend this book to be both instructional and informative. Analysts will learn how to produce risk terrain models and maps that give actionable meaning to the relationships that exist between place-based indicators and crime outcomes, and to diagnose the spatial attractors of chronically criminogenic places. Planners will learn how to use RTM strategically to forecast where crime problems are likely to emerge and how to engage in steps that might reduce the risk of crime occurring in the future. We have been told that part of the reason our work has been widely adopted is not only because we have successfully demonstrated how to bring this research into the policy arena but also because we have shown how it can be specifically applied to informing and managing operations in a day-to-day context. The future will tell how important RTM will be in furthering crime analysis, forecasting, and prevention. But we hope this book will provide readers with a solid basis upon which to advance RTM methods and apply RTM in innovative and meaningful ways to their own topics of interest.

In chapters 1 through 5, we present RTM in the context of past criminological research. We explain how this idea has developed over the last six years, specifically the origins of the idea, the evolution of the concept of spatial influence as it informs how we examine risk factors and their impact on crime, and the technical steps in building risk terrain models. All of this will lead to a discussion of the Theory of Risky Places. In chapters 6 through 8, we operationalize the Theory of Risky Places and present practical applications of risk terrain models in informing police agencies. We explain how risky places are best understood when interpreted within event contexts, and we present best practices for risk management and ACTION (Assessment, Connections, Tasks, Interventions, Outcomes, and Notifications).

ACKNOWLEDGMENTS

We would like to thank all of our colleagues, students, and practitioner partners who have worked with us to advance RTM methods and complete research projects over the last few years. We have been fortunate to benefit from their collective wisdom and talents, and are proud to share with the readers of this book the insightful products of our collaborations. A very special thank you to Eric Piza for helping us define important parameters of RTM and articulate its practical applications to crime analysis and policing. Eric began working with us early in this enterprise and has become a full partner in our research and scholarship. We are also lucky to have him as a friend. And to Chris Andreychak, thank you for, early on, helping to shape and embolden our current research trajectory. Our work has been enthusiastically supported by Rutgers University and its School of Criminal Justice, and the Rutgers Center on Public Security, for which we are very grateful. We are also very appreciative of the financial support we have repeatedly received from the National Institute of Justice, and Joel Hunt's guidance and encouragement as well. We thank the entire team at the University of California Press, including the reviewers, who have been enthusiastic about this project and expended the effort and resources to successfully complete this book.

Les Kennedy, as always, would like to acknowledge the ongoing support and encouragement of his family members, Ilona, Alexis, Andrea, Stu, Espen, Alex, and Helga. They have rallied around me for years in treating my work as interesting and important, a wonderful present that I continue to enjoy in my never boring career. I would also like to give a special thanks to Joel, who has become a close friend, as well as a valued colleague. His special talents have made our work come alive and his courage in tackling hard problems is inspirational. I am grateful that we have had this time to work together and look forward to many years of discovery and problem solving to come.

Joel Caplan would like to acknowledge the loving support and encouragement of his family members, Oranit, Oriellah, and Shailee. Their ability to help me achieve a healthy balance of work and play is such a treasured gift that allows me to pursue my professional goals while also enjoying the journey. I am a better person and scholar because of you all. Thank you so much for being so amazing. I would also like to thank Les. He has long been my mentor and now I am truly honored to call him a colleague and friend. Together, we have realized that scholarship can have so many rewards beyond their immediate intended results. Thank you for your honest opinions and confidence in our partnership; I look forward to continuing to work together to change the world.

PROLOGUE

Our collaboration in developing and advancing risk terrain modeling (RTM) has led to a truly exhilarating set of achievements. Since 2009, we have been applying RTM to advance research on the spatial dynamics of crime. Products from this research have been presented at professional conferences, including the American Society of Criminology (ASC), the International Association of Crime Analysts (IACA), the International Association of Chiefs of Police (IACP), and several separate events sponsored by the National Institute of Justice, the Department of Homeland Security, the White House, and other organizations throughout the world. RTM research has been published in leading refereed journals and edited books. In March 2012, our inaugural publication in *Justice Quarterly* (Caplan, Kennedy, & Miller, 2011) received the Donal MacNamara Award for Outstanding Journal Publication from the Academy of Criminal Justice Sciences (ACJS). In September 2013 we were truly honored to receive the IACA Membership Award for an "outstanding contribution to the crime analysis profession." An article in *Forbes* published in October 2014 (Acharya, 2014) ranked RTM in the top 5 list of "big data" used for social good.

We developed the RTMDx Utility (discussed in this book) in 2012 to automate RTM methods. This avenue of research and software development aids in the creation of "expert systems technologies," which emulate criminal justice practitioners' cognitive processes to inform the actions of nonexpert analysts and enhance their performance without requiring the same investment in time and resources. Largely due to our open-access policy (that is, most resources are available through www.riskterrainmodeling

.com), RTM methods have been adopted by academic colleagues and public safety practitioners internationally, including Chicago, New York, Paris, Milan, and Bogotá; RTM is used on every continent on Earth (except Antarctica).

There have been independent tests of RTM by others who have confirmed that our statistical approach is sound. We are also aware of a growing body of peer-reviewed publications by authors unaffiliated with us who have utilized RTM methods. Academics and analysts alike have subscribed to our webinar in large numbers since it was first offered in 2011. We have received funding from major federal agencies to develop RTM-based interventions in collaboration with police department partners and to conduct evaluations of outcomes. We discuss some of this research in this book. More recently, we have begun collaborations with professionals in disciplines outside of criminology, such as engineering and biology, who have introduced us to new ways of using computational approaches that are complementary to our current practices to study crime.

We are humbled by the response to RTM among both academicians and professional practitioners, and remain confident in our approach to its development and application, since it is so firmly based on solid foundations of criminological research. Our interactions with city officials and stakeholders while conducting research, from major metropolitan areas to smaller suburban and rural towns, demonstrate that people love to problem-solve, and this is exactly what RTM promotes. This book was written as we reflected on the early achievements of RTM, while looking forward to its continued evolution. We intend this book to synthesize and interpret our work to date on RTM and to share with criminologists, police officers, crime and intelligence analysts, geographers, GIS professionals, and other public safety practitioners the current state of RTM based on empirical results and scientific insights.

EXPLAINING THE CONTEXTS
OF CRIME

THE PATTERNS AND PERSISTENCE OF CRIME

Criminal behavior is best understood as a social product that occurs in a patterned fashion, rarely fluctuating wildly from time to time or place to place. This observation was first made 170 years ago by Quetelet (1984). We believe that this enduring pattern occurs because the underlying factors that increase or decrease the risk of crime are not quick to change and exert fairly consistent effects on the appearance, distribution, and persistence of crime by attracting illegal behavior. However, although this pattern appears to be fairly regular, if not chronic, over time at the aggregate level, there are many factors that contribute on the micro level to the ever-changing landscape of crime incidents. Of interest to us here are how these factors may combine to encourage crime to start, how they affect the momentum of crime events over time, and how they can be manipulated to make crime stop.

The ideas that were developed and discussed by Quetelet and others about the origins and persistence of crime took on new urgency with the massive growth of American cities at the turn of the twentieth century, due to large waves of immigrants who began to flow into the United States and other Western countries. These migrants brought about changes in urban areas that caught the attention of researchers who were concerned about the negative impact that this rapid growth was having on communities. The consequences for urban planning, social reform, and economic transactions were transformative. Accompanying these changes were new concerns about crime and delinquency. In the heady days of urban research that ensued, Clifford Shaw and Henry McKay began to map urban areas and emphasized contextual factors related to delinquency. Shaw and McKay (1969) used this contextual mapping approach to document the areas in which crime had persisted over time.

Human ecologists (Park, McKenzie, & Burgess, 1925) talked about "natural areas," a term that appeared in studies of delinquency in Chicago in the early twentieth century. Natural areas, according to these researchers, were settings that had certain characteristics that led to predictable behavioral outcomes. Shaw and McKay reported through methodical observation that "natural areas" in Chicago appeared constant over time. They plotted delinquency incidents in Chicago over many decades and found that they concentrated in "transitional" zones. In addition, they reported that crime declined as one moved from the inner-city areas to the (outer) suburbs. A key observation from their research was that community characteristics and problems (for example, cultural conflict, gang behavior, conflict with families) stayed the same despite the changing attributes of the inhabitants (Hatt, 1946). As people came from and went into these areas, the social disorder and delinquency remained high, despite changes in the ethnic composition of inhabitants. Oddly, despite the importance of Shaw and McKay's finding that community characteristics matter for delinquency and its reduction and prevention, they overlooked it in their prescriptions for addressing the delinquency problems that interested them. They suggested instead that the behavior of people in these areas defined their qualities despite the physical characteristics that these areas exhibited. As Snodgrass points out:

> To interpret their findings, Shaw and McKay relied most heavily upon the general concept of "social disorganization," the breakdown of social controls in the "communities" located in the transitional zone. The invasion by business and industries from the center of the city into the former residential areas created a wake of social disorganization in its advance which disturbed social cohesion and disrupted traditional conduct norms. Shaw and McKay explicitly and repeatedly mentioned industrial invasion as a primary source of communal disorganisation, although other sources, e.g. the influx of successive waves of highly mobile immigrant groups, were additional contributing factors, though not unrelated to business expansion. (Snodgrass, 1976, p. 9)

Their emphasis on social disorganization made sense to Shaw and McKay as social activists who believed that the causes of delinquency resided within the local traditions and cultural values of the inhabitants, even though, again, they were quick to point out that as different groups passed through these areas (particularly the zone of transition), the problems of delinquency and social disorder persisted. In other words, the factors that stayed consistent in these areas, that is, businesses and other physical features, were treated as tangential to the ways in which delinquency emerged and areas deteriorated.

As Snodgrass further points out:

A most striking aspect of Shaw and McKay's interpretation, then, is the absence of attempts to link business and industrial invasion with the causes of delinquency. The interpretation stayed at the communal level and turned inward to find the causes of delinquency in internal conditions and process within the socially disorganized area. Thus, their interpretation stopped abruptly at the point at which the relationship between industrial expansion and high delinquency areas could have gone beyond the depiction of the two as coincidentally adjacent to one another geographically. (p. 10)

In fact, Shaw and McKay did not see proximity to industry and commerce as causal but rather simply as an index of the areas where delinquency would be located. This failure to account for the effects of community characteristics, or environmental features, in attracting illegal behavior and spurring crime is surprising, given their huge effort in identifying spatial patterns of delinquency through mapping incidents, a project that went on for over 40 years.

Bursik (1988) points out that stability in ecological influence stayed constant before World War II in Chicago but changed thereafter, thus affording the opportunity to compare how these ecological factors influenced criminal behavior. In addition, generalizing the influence of environmental factors to the experience in other cities was hard to achieve and led to criticisms that Shaw and McKay's approach was not replicable (p. 526). But the observation that environmental factors can influence the nature of places is important and should not be lost in the disappointment concerning the inability to replicate Shaw and McKay's findings within Chicago over time or in another city in a predictable fashion. The external validity problem appears to originate not from the conceptualization of the importance of environment but from the limitations in the methodology used to measure its effects. It also derives from a fixation on the actors in crime rather than a consideration of them in the spatial contexts in which they operate, a divergence in approach since Shaw and McKay's time that has persisted in crime research until recently.

So, despite their reliance on maps and time series data to illustrate crime persistence, Shaw and McKay did not fully explicate how environment ties to crime emergence or outcome. There are conceptual and methodological reasons for this that we will explore below. It should be noted that Shaw and McKay's assumptions concerning the importance of the links between neighborhood characteristics and crime have been extensively studied using a social disorganization perspective that concentrates on the ways in which social control manifests itself in certain locations, typified by poverty and high levels of in-and-out migration. In particular, the work of Shevky and Bell (1955) examined the ways in which family status, socioeconomic characteristics, and ethnicity combined to influence behavioral outcomes using social area analysis. Social area analysis improved on the inflexibility of the idea of natural areas by combining community features through the way that they overlapped in different locations (Hatt, 1946; Heitgerd & Bursik, 1987; Janson, 1980). (See figure 1.) The areas of overlap were considered the locations in which crime problems would be greater.

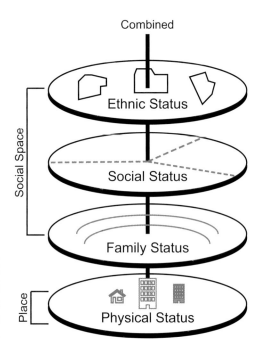

FIGURE 1
(Adapted from Murdie, 1969). Urban social space constructs and their territorial relationships to physical space. Social area analysts combined community features through the way they overlapped in space.

Unfortunately for social area analysts, as was the case with the ecologists who preceded them, they were unable to move beyond macrolevel explanations for delinquency outcomes in spatial terms based on the underlying characteristics in the study area. Their multilevel approach was novel, however, and was adopted by urban planners such as McHarg (1995) to help depict the concentration of features in a landscape.

Recent work on social disorganization has focused on the ways in which areas suffering from social and physical disorders respond through collective efficacy—the pooling together of efforts to extract resources to battle problems faced in neighborhoods (Morenoff, Sampson, & Raudenbush, 2001). This work has provided an important stimulus for community planners to think more broadly about how community empowerment can be used to combat serious consequences of disorganization. Operating at the community or neighborhood level allows for a comprehensive assessment of local well-being and elicits steps that can be taken to address inequality and social upheaval. However, this research still relies on aggregate statistics and tends not to account for the physical environment as a major factor, at the microlevel, in bringing about criminogenic conditions that regularly attract illegal behavior.

THE GEOGRAPHY FOR CRIME

Helping to overcome the limitations outlined above, improvements in data collection and advanced mapping technology have opened up the possibility of better microlevel analysis of places and crime. However, with advances in geospatial approaches, the ways that features of a landscape have been modeled in a geographic information system (GIS) are often contrary to how people experience and conceptualize their environments (Couclelis, 1992; Frank & Mark, 1991). Geographers suggest that regions, such as cities, are learned piecemeal rather than imagined whole by humans over time, an assertion that is grounded in views from psychology (Freundschuh & Egenhofer, 1997; Montello, 1993). So when assessing the likelihood or risk of crime occurring at conceivably any location throughout a city landscape, vector objects in a GIS (for example, points that are used to represent things such as bars, schools, or bus stops) are poor representations of criminogenic features on a map because they bear no particular relationship to the dynamic environments of which they are a part (Couclelis, 1992). "There are difficulties with this view of the world," explained Couclelis (1992, p. 66), "mainly that points, lines, and polygons that define vector objects do not have naturally occurring counterparts in the real world." They are approximations of environmental features, but without any theoretical or empirical link to their geographies (Freundschuh & Egenhofer, 1997).

Broad inattention to different spatial conceptualizations of criminogenic features by crime researchers has led to misrepresentations of these urban, suburban, and rural features in geographic information systems and resulting maps (Freundschuh & Egenhofer, 1997). The way people (for example, motivated offenders or suitable victims) conceptualize and operate in space is an important consideration for the mapping of the risk of crime throughout landscapes. Cartographically modeling these conceptualizations and the spatial influences of criminogenic features in a GIS in a way that reflects the actors' views is an important part of what Freundschuh and Egenhofer (1997, p. 363) describe as "Naïve Geography, a set of theories of how people intuitively or spontaneously conceptualize geographic space and time" (Egenhofer & Mark, 1995). It can yield more meaningful inferences about criminal behavior and actionable spatial intelligence for use by public safety professionals (Frank, 1993; Mark, 1993; Freundschuh & Egenhofer, 1997). Spatial risks for crime must be considered in terms of how the environment forms behavior.

CONCEPTUALIZING SPATIAL CRIME RISKS

We will use the concepts of "space," "place," and "area" (and variations thereof, for example, "spatial") deliberately throughout this book. So to clarify: "Space" is defined as a continuous expanse within which things exist and move. "Place" is a particular portion of space where defined activities or functions may occur. A place is the microlevel unit of analysis for risk terrain modeling (RTM). An "area" is a part of space defined as two or more contingent places.

Examining places rather than people for crime analysis does not remove the importance of the human factor. It simply shifts the focus away from personal characteristics to personal preferences. How individual persons select and use the environments that they occupy and the impact that this has on crime outcomes become the direct focus of the spatial risk perspective. This approach to crime analysis suggests a way of looking at behavioral outcomes less as deterministic and more as a function of a dynamic interaction among people that occurs at places. The attributes of places that we seek to identify are not constant, nor necessarily are the interactions set in place over time. However, the ways in which these factors combine can be studied to reveal consistent patterns of interaction that align with the view expressed by Brantingham and Brantingham (1981) in their development of crime pattern theory.

Risk provides a metric that can help tie different parts of a crime problem together and offers a probabilistic interpretation for crime analysis that allows us to suggest that certain things are likely to happen and others can be prevented according to our risk assessments (Kennedy & Van Brunschot, 2009, p. 11). Risk is based on a consideration of the probabilities of particular outcomes. When opportunity for crime is thought of in terms of "risk of crime," places can be evaluated in terms of varying degrees of criminogenic risk relative to certain nearby or faraway features of the environment (Cohen, Kluegel, & Land, 1981; Caplan, 2011). Again, this directs attention away from a fixation on only the offender or victim in responses to crime and permits considerations of characteristics of places as well.

In their simplest form, place-based interventions lead to strategies that direct police to particular areas to use the tools most directly available to them to solve problems, such as arrests or summonses targeted at people located there. But this approach is incomplete. Problem-oriented policing has offered important clues on how we can change situations to make them less conducive to crime (Mastrofski, Weisburd, & Braga, 2010). In this regard it is important to address the collective influence of certain spatial features as a principal approach to crime prevention. In arguing for improving how we study crime events, Braga and Clarke (2014) present a compelling justification for studies of places that focus on risks associated with certain types of environmental features. These features can create opportunities for crime, attract offenders, enable illegal behavior, and confound agents of social control in containing or suppressing their negative effects. But, at the same time, an understanding of an environmental feature's relative importance in creating risk of crime, as well as an understanding of how to target these features, can offer geographically focused strategies for crime prevention. The spatial risk perspective not only addresses the role that changing situational factors might have on a crime outcome, but also evaluates the overall effect of addressing the relative risks presented by features that have strong spatial influences on criminal behavior. With RTM, we can identify these features and their interaction with others in creating risky places. These places should be key targets for change and crime prevention.

Brantingham and Brantingham (1995) argue that spatial crime patterns, and their stability over time, are a function of the environmental backcloth of the area under study. The Brantinghams suggest that this backcloth is dotted with "crime attractors" and "crime generators." Attractors include features of the environment that entice offenders to places to commit crime. Generators, meanwhile, are represented by increased opportunities for crime that emerge from the collection of more people into areas following specific types of behavior, simply because of the increased volume of interaction taking place in these areas. This work by the Brantinghams reconnects an interest in physical environments to human criminal behavior. The recent works on crime places revisit this interest in environment and crime (see Weisburd, Groff, & Yang, 2012; Johnson, Bowers, Birks, & Pease, 2008), and the innovative view of "place as case" suggests that if crime can be seen as situationally located it is more likely to be mitigated and prevented (Lum & Koper, 2013). The interest in environmental effects on crime as presented in this literature reinforces the view that certain places are riskier than others. Testing how risk is distributed across spaces requires methods that accommodate the combined effects of many factors at once, as was the original intent of social area analysts. However, key to our current understanding of how factors combine are the concept of "spatial influence" and the advanced reasoning around the operationalization of this influence through measures of distance and density within a GIS (see Caplan, 2011).

Recent research on spatial crime risk has benefited from increased sophistication in the ways in which cartographic representations of crime incidents can be made with readily available data and GIS functionalities, overcoming the limitations of vector-based applications, discussed above (Tomlin, 1994). Geographic information systems have allowed analysts access to data that have been routinely acquired in cities for purposes other than crime analysis (for example, determining land use or plotting electoral maps). Combined, these data allow the development of composite views of landscapes that can be used to consider how places differ in terms of the risk they pose in fostering crime. But as Freundschuh and Egenhofer (1997) remind us, combining municipal features data regarding how they relate to human behavior is not straightforward because it is not simply the physical presence of features that defines risky places, but also their spatial influences.

SPATIAL INFLUENCE

Spatial influence refers to the way in which features of an environment affect behaviors at or around the features themselves. It serves as the measurable link between features of a landscape and their impacts on people and the ways in which they use space. Spatial influence is, essentially, the articulation of perceptual cues observed from features and gleaned from personal opinions, experiences, and empirical knowledge about similar features or characteristics thereof under other similar circumstances (Downs & Stea, 1973; Fuhrmann, Huynh, & Scholz, 2013). Perceptual cues used to articulate spatial influences of features may be positive, negative, or something in between. Perceptions may differ between individuals, but collectively, in reference to certain times and settings, patterns emerge and can be operationalized in a GIS. For example, a sidewalk and a bush might be considered benign features of any generic landscape. But a sidewalk located in an isolated and poorly lit section of a college campus that is lined on both sides by many tall bushes could be considered by students as a risky area (Fisher & Nasar, 1995; Furhmann et al., 2013; Hites et al., 2013; Tseng, Duane, & Hadipriono, 2004). Here, the spatial influence of sidewalks might be defined as "being within a certain distance from the sidewalk increases my risk of victimization because offenders presume that people are likely to travel on them." The spatial influence of bushes could be defined as "being within a high concentration of tall bushes increases my risk of victimization because it allows many places for motivated offenders to hide." In this way, sidewalks could be depicted in a GIS not as finite lines to represent paths, but as areas accounting for all places within, for example, 25 feet of sidewalks. Bushes could be depicted in a GIS according to kernel density calculations.

Operationalizing the spatial influences of features of a landscape to GIS maps complements what Freundschuh, Engenhofer, Couclelis, and other geographers advocated for when measuring the theoretical and behavioral links between people and their geographies. Most basically, it maximizes the construct validity of cartographic models and empirical measures used for statistical tests (Golledge & Stimson, 1997). It allows us to consistently evaluate places relative to one another with regard to the types of behaviors we would expect given the influences that certain features have on people located there.

We can infer that the risk of crime is exceptionally high at places where the spatial influences of particular features colocate, such as a secluded pedestrian corridor defined as an area within 25 feet of a sidewalk and a high density of bushy plants. Some students may prefer to avoid this area, while motivated offenders may be attracted to it (Lane, Gover, & Dahod, 2009; Woolnaugh, 2009). This is why lamps, "blue light" emergency call boxes, or CCTV cameras are directed by college administrators to these areas: because the positive spatial influences of these "protective" features are often intended to mitigate risk perceptions.

In other examples, how might a house's proximity to high schools increase risk of residential burglary? Or what might be the spatial influence of bars on the risks of robbery? How would you operationalize the spatial influence of other features of the landscape, such as automated teller machines (ATMs), with regard to robbery risk? Spatial influence research suggests that in looking for the relationship between notable features of a landscape and crime, we should be aware that these features, or their effects, might differ by type of crime. The spatial influence of ATMs on robbery could be quite different than their spatial influence on bicycle theft, for instance. The existing empirical research literature should be reviewed to identify what features may be relevant to each crime type in the jurisdiction under study, and to inform decisions about how to operationalize spatial influences. As we said, there is an extensive literature on key factors that correlate with crime outcomes. Many of these studies and ways of accessing them will be discussed in this book. Professional practitioner insights also play a valuable role in this process.

So, spatial influence is the articulable affect of an environmental feature on human behavior (see Andresen, 2014, p. 180; Jacobs, 1961/1992; Alexiou, 2006). The relative risks that manifest spatial influences allow us to compute a probability of criminal behavior occurring. In other words, a place's vulnerability to crime is operationalized by the spatial influences of nearby features. This spatial vulnerability is based on the idea that everything relates to everything else, but things that are closer are more related (Tobler, 1970). If this is true (in terms of both promoting and discouraging certain types of behavior), then the cumulative effects of spatial influences should be such that certain places within the spatial influence of multiple criminogenic features would be more vulnerable to crime than places that are not influenced by one or more criminogenic features. RTM creates this composite model and related map of spatial vulnerabilities to crime at places throughout a landscape.

SPATIAL VULNERABILITIES AND CRIME

Crime incidents could conceivably occur at any place throughout space since criminals do not generally offend with regard to census tracts or other common macrogeographic units. A victim who was shot at 123 Main Street could just as likely have been shot at 115 Main Street if he stopped to tie his shoe, walked slower, or was delayed for any number of other reasons. To model such a continuous surface of possible crime places, equally sized cells that compose a grid covering the entire study setting are the standard unit of analysis for RTM. Raster mapping in a GIS was specifically developed to model geographic spaces, or landscapes, in this way (Tomlin, 1991, 1994), and is ideally suited to capture the reality of how people operate within a landscape. It is very good for modeling how crime can occur at microlevel units (Groff & La Vigne, 2002). Cells of a raster grid can be the microlevel units of analysis for RTM.

Technically, cell sizes determine how coarse or smooth the raster map will appear: the smaller the cell size, the smoother the map (imagine pixels on a television screen). Conceptually, raster cells are the operational definition of "places." Their size is generally determined to be the smallest meaningful place for crime events to happen within. A cell size of half the mean block length in a city might be selected because it allows us to model places for crime occurrence at approximately one corner (or the other) of a block face. It is also likely to be the smallest spatial unit to which police could reasonably be deployed.

We developed RTM to identify and describe vulnerable places and to make forecasts of future crime incident locations that do not rely solely on the occurrence of past incidences. This is achieved by diagnosing the common environmental correlates of spatial crime patterns and identifying the risks that manifest these factors or features. RTM models how the spatial influences of criminogenic features colocate to create unique behavior settings for crime. With RTM we infer the risk of crime from the combined spatial influences of certain features of the landscape to produce actionable intelligence for intervention strategies directed at the risk factors at places, with the goal of mitigating their spatial influences. Risk-based intervention strategies will be discussed in chapters 7 and 8.

Thus far in this book, you should understand that RTM is a framework for studying spatial crime vulnerability, and that spatial influence is a foundational concept for understanding and applying this framework. Spatial inference suggests that we are able to extract from a risk terrain model meaningful information for understanding criminal behavior patterns, for diagnosing attractors of existing crime clusters, and for forecasting places where new crimes are likely to emerge. Such information enables the production of spatial intelligence, which is the communication and application of spatial inferences for deliberate action. Detailed technical steps of RTM are discussed in the next chapter.

2

RISK TERRAIN MODELING METHODS

As we discussed in the last chapter, we are interested foremost in the spatial influence of risk factors in the environment on crime outcomes. Our work over the last few years has been directed at operationalizing these relationships in a theoretically informed way and applying proper statistical tests to establish the probabilities that crimes will occur in certain places. The development of risk terrain modeling (RTM) has been set into the context of an ongoing debate about the value of evidence-based approaches to policing and the viability of "predictive" modeling in informing police strategies and tactics (Perry, McInnis, Price, Smith, & Hollywood, 2013). The result has been the merging together of key concepts from environmental criminology and spatial analysis. The product is a technically sophisticated and theoretically grounded approach to spatial crime analysis. In this chapter, we articulate how RTM has been operationalized through a series of steps that forms an applied method of concept development, operationalization, analysis, and applications in an organized and systematic fashion. These steps guide the further elaboration of the method in chapters that follow.

RTM is a systematic plan of action for studying spatial vulnerability to crime. We say that crime is the outcome event because that is the focus of this book. But we know of RTM being applied to a variety of other topics, such as injury prevention, public health, child maltreatment, traffic accidents, pollution studies, urban development, and homeland security. RTM refers to three key processes: (1) standardizing disparate datasets to a common geography, (2) diagnosing spatial risk factors, and (3) articulating spatial vulnerabilities. The first is a cartographic process of operationalizing qualities of a landscape to geographic maps. These map layers represent the spatial influences of environmental factors across places. The second is a deliberate and often statistically informed process of identifying and weighting factors that geographically relate to crime incidents. The third is an empirical and cartographic process whereby the spatial influences of these environmental factors are combined to communicate information about spatial contexts for crime (that is, spatial vulnerabilitics). RTM offers a statistically valid way to articulate vulnerable places. Risk values of places derived from RTM do not suggest the inevitability of crime. Instead, they point to locations where the likelihood of criminal behavior will be high.

The steps of RTM are not complicated, although some of the analysis can appear technically challenging. We will present an overview here to illustrate how we intend the modeling process to be used, keeping the technical steps as accessible to the reader as possible. Additional resources are available at www.riskterrainmodeling.com. RTM is straightforward for people with basic skillsets in a geographic information system (GIS). To make RTM more accessible to a broad audience of researchers and practitioners, Rutgers University developed the Risk Terrain Modeling Diagnostics (RTMDx) Utility, a desktop software app (Caplan & Kennedy, 2013) that automates most steps of RTM.[1] The RTMDx Utility tests a variety of spatial influences for every input factor to identify the most empirically and theoretically grounded spatial associations with known crime incident locations. Then, it empirically selects only the most appropriate risk factors (with their spatial influences optimally operationalized) to produce a "best" risk terrain model. The final model articulates the spatial vulnerability for crime with relative risk scores at every place throughout the study area, based on the spatial influence of each significant environmental risk factor. The factors that create specific vulnerabilities at places are weighted according to their relative spatial influences on crime events. This aids in crime forecasting and the prioritization of risk mitigation efforts, as will be discussed in more detail in this book. This chapter explains the current state of RTM methods, including a summary of the technical steps and statistical procedures that are actualized by the RTMDx Utility.

There are 10 steps to risk terrain modeling:

1. choose an outcome event;
2. choose a study area;
3. choose a time period;
4. identify best available (possible) risk factors;
5. obtain spatial data;
6. map spatial influence of factors;
7. select model factors;
8. weight model factors;
9. quantitatively combine model factors;
10. communicate meaningful information.

CASE STUDY ILLUSTRATING THE STEPS OF RTM

A demonstrative case study, based on a research project funded by the National Institute of Justice,[2] in collaboration with Eric Piza, applies RTM to robbery in Kansas City, Missouri, using readily accessible resources and administrative data. In addition to Kansas City being the setting for the current case study, it is also well known in criminal justice circles for the Kansas City Preventative Patrol Experiment, a landmark study conducted between 1972 and 1973.

STEPS 1, 2, AND 3

This case study is intended to diagnose the underlying spatial attractors of robberies (that is, step 1) throughout the landscape of Kansas City (that is, step 2) during calendar year 2012 (that is, step 3). Robberies in Kansas City do, in fact, cluster at specific areas. But robberies, or any other crime types, could become endemic without any evidence of significant spatial clustering of incidents; assault and battery to police officers, which will be discussed in chapter 6, is one such example of this happenstance. The question to be answered with RTM, then, is: Regardless of whether crime incidents cluster spatially, do they share common spatial correlates of the landscape upon which they occur? The sections that follow address steps 4 through 10, which answer this question.

GENERAL COMMENTARY FOR STEPS 1–3

RTM is specifically tailored to the outcome event of interest. Because different crimes have unique and sometimes different underlying causes/attractors/generators, separate models should be produced for each crime type.

RTM can be applied to any geographic extent (that is, local, regional, global; urban, suburban, rural; land, sea). Select an area for which the information provided by the risk terrain model and related maps will be meaningful and actionable (for example, citywide jurisdiction, police sector, and the like). Use data that is representative of the entire study area. This may include risk factor data that is outside the study area boundary, but whose spatial influences could extend into the study area.

The time period should be meaningful for the data used and considerate of how the information communicated by the risk terrain model's output and any related maps will be used for decision making. Here, the calendar year 2012 time period diagnoses the spatial features common to the settings where robbery incidents occurred, while "controlling" for seasonality since the year worth of data generalizes across all seasons. An RTM for robberies on or around a college campus might use a September through May time period. Or a police department task force interested in addressing robberies during the holiday season may focus on the months of November and December, as was done for a police intervention conducted in Arlington, Texas (Edmonds & Mallard, 2011). For crime diagnostics, use input data that are most representative of the features of the landscape as they were for the time period of the outcome event data being used.

POSSIBLE RISK FACTORS (STEP 4)

The product of this step should be a comprehensive list of factors potentially related to the robbery outcome events. Two approaches were used to identify the "pool" of risk factors tested for inclusion in this risk terrain model:

(1) Existing empirical research literature was reviewed to identify a variety of factors that have been found to correlate with robbery. The sources of this review included library catalogues and electronic journal databases, Google Scholar, reports and other grey literature, and resources from reputable agencies and professional organizations (such as the US Department of Justice, Pew, Campbell, and the International Association of Crime Analysts).

(2) Professional and practitioner insights also played an invaluable role in determining which factors are likely relevant for this particular jurisdiction. The knowledge of Kansas City Police Department (KCPD) personnel provided practical, experience-based justification for the use of some factors in this study. Jurisdictions throughout the world have specific crime problems that relate to a unique set of factors that may be best identified by local officials who work in these environments on a regular basis. As a consequence of our approach to identifying possible risk factors, our factor candidate pool is not only empirically driven but also theoretically and practically meaningful. Factors identified for use in this case study are: rental halls, bowling alleys, coffee shops, convenience stores, foreclosures, gas stations, gas stations with convenience stores, grocery stores, health care centers and gyms, Laundromats, parking stations, pawnshops, take-out restaurants, sit-down restaurants, sports arenas, variety stores, libraries, schools, banks, bars, drug markets, hotels, parks, weapon offending parolees and probationers, suspicious persons with weapon calls-for-service, movie theaters, packaged liquor stores, liquor licensed retailers, nightclubs, and strip clubs.

This broad spectrum of factors, or features of a landscape, identified from a variety of sources, may attract illegal behavior and pose general spatial risks resulting in robbery outcomes. However, it is likely that only some of these factors will be significantly influential within Kansas City specifically. Therefore, it is hypothesized that (1) certain features of the physical environment will constitute significantly higher risk of robbery at places than others. Furthermore, (2) the copresence of one or more spatial influences of risky features at places will have higher risk of robbery incidents compared to places absent said features' spatial influences.

OBTAINING SPATIAL DATA (STEP 5)

RTM relies on valid and reliable data sources. Data used for this study were collected from the KCPD and InfoGroup, a data and marketing services company that provides detailed information about public entities. Although much of the data needed for RTM are of public record, accessing them from each of the various agencies within Kansas

City was not feasible, so we decided to purchase them from InfoGroup. For people using RTM in jurisdictions that have GIS data clearinghouses or public data portals, most data can be obtained easily for free. While data may be obtainable from various external sources, "internal" sources (that is, city agencies or departments) can have better, more up-to-date land use information, so be sure to carefully consider all sourcing options. The risk factor data sets obtained from InfoGroup at the address level included rental halls, bowling alleys, coffee shops, convenience stores, foreclosures, gas stations, gas stations with convenience stores, grocery stores, health care centers and gyms, Laundromats, parking stations, pawnshops, take-out restaurants, sit-down restaurants, sports arenas, and variety stores. Crime and some other datasets were provided at the address level by the KCPD: robbery incidents, libraries, schools, banks, bars, drug markets, hotels, parks, weapon offending parolees and probationers, suspicious persons with weapon calls-for-service, movie theaters, packaged liquor stores, liquor licensed retailers, nightclubs, and strip clubs. A polygon shapefile (base map) of the city boundary was provided by KCPD.

Once a list of potential risk factor data sets was compiled, visual inspection of the data in a GIS was used to "get to know" the data and to explore which features appear to colocate with (or share similar patterns of) robbery incident locations. Using a GIS, each potential risk factor data set was layered, respectively, with point features of robbery incidents and visually inspected for possible spatial relationships. Features that generally appeared to share a spatial relationship were selected for (statistical validity) testing. Mostly, this process was used to *exclude* factors that very obviously did not appear to spatially relate to the robbery incidents in order to create a more parsimonious model for the Kansas City jurisdiction.

GENERAL COMMENTARY FOR STEP 5

RTM was developed to leverage data from various sources and use readily accessible methods that most people could replicate. In our own work, we have reviewed library databases and open-research publications from the US Department of Justice and other outlets, including Google Scholar, to identify possible risk factors and obtain related datasets for many different crime types. We have also obtained base maps of, for example, roads and city outlines from the US Geological Survey or the Census Bureau when police departments or other city agencies do not have them. Crime and risk factor datasets must be particular to the study settings. Increasingly in the United States, these data can be downloaded from open sources like Open Data Philly, the Chicago Data Portal, or the Florida Geographic Data Library.

Content validity and construct validity are especially important when preparing data and considering data sources for RTM. Content validity refers to the degree to which a dataset represents all facets of a given construct. For the construct of "elementary schools," for example, a dataset with school names and addresses obtained from the Department of Education may lack content validity if it only contains public schools, excluding private and charter schools. Or if it begins at first grade and misses kindergartens. An element of subjectivity exists in relation to determining content validity. Be sure to operationally define your factor and know your data!

Construct validity refers to the degree to which inferences can legitimately be made from the operational definitions of your factors to the theoretical constructs on which those operationalizations were based. Construct validity is related to generalizing from your factor concept to the factor measures. A potential risk factor (identified in step 4) is a "construct" and the feature dataset is your operationalization of that construct. When thinking of data sources for RTM in this way, we are talking about the construct validity of the datasets. The dataset is how you translate a risk factor construct into an operationalized measure for testing and modeling.

To illustrate, consider the "bar." The intent of this construct is likely a liquor establishment with on-site consumption (as opposed to a take-out packaged goods store). The theoretical framework of the link between bars and robbery could be that intoxicated patrons are more susceptible to robbery because they are less able to resist or fight back. So, what dataset would you use as a valid measure? Would you include any business that serves liquor for on-site consumption, including hotels or restaurants, such as the Cheesecake Factory? Would you include nightclubs, where patrons go primarily to dance but also to consume liquor? Or would you include only pubs or taverns where people go primarily to drink? There is no correct answer, but the decision should be made thoughtfully according to how you believe the construct of bars is theoretically linked to the criminal behavior that you are interested in studying. Select datasets that get directly at the operational definition of your risk factor construct. Construct validity is essential for interpreting results from RTM and for planning appropriate interventions to mitigate risks in a direct fashion.

The jurisdiction of Kansas City was modeled as a grid of 462ft by 462ft cells (N = 42,814), with each cell representing a place throughout the city. Four hundred sixty-two feet approximates the average block length in Kansas City, as measured within a GIS. This spatial dimension has practical meaning since the cell size corresponds to the block face of Kansas City's street network, representing the most realistic unit for police deployment at the micro level (Kennedy, Caplan, & Piza, 2011). Moreover, empirical research by Taylor and Harrell (1996) suggests that "behavior settings" are crime-prone places that typically comprise just a few street blocks (Taylor, 1988).

To determine the optimal spatial influence of each risky feature, several maps were operationalized from the 30 aforementioned potential risk factors of the Kansas City landscape. For each risk factor, we measured whether each cell in the grid was within 462ft, 924ft, or 1386ft of a feature point, or in an area of high density of the feature points based on a kernel density bandwidth of 462ft, 924ft, or 1386ft. These distances represent approximately 1 block, 2 blocks, and 3 blocks in Kansas City, and are intended to model vulnerability connected to the features within these areas. Grid cells within the city's study extent that were inside each Euclidean distance threshold were represented as 1 (highest risk); cells outside this distance were represented as 0 (not highest risk). Density variables were reclassified into highest density (density ≥ mean + 2 standard deviations) and not highest density (density < mean + 2 standard deviations) regions. Cells within the highest-density regions were represented with a value of 1; cells not within the highest-density regions were represented with a value of 0. We used the RTMDx Utility (Caplan & Kennedy, 2013) to automate this process for each potential risk factor and then assemble all of these values into a table where rows represented cells within the Kansas City study area grid and columns represented binary values (that is, 1 or 0, as just described above), accordingly. Counts of robbery incidents located within each cell were also recorded (for subsequent statistical testing, which is discussed in the next step).

In truth, we did not actually instruct the RTMDx Utility to operationalize every single one of the 180 possible risk maps (that is, 2 operationalizations of spatial influence * up to 3 blocks * 30 factors). Instructions were customized for each factor using the "nearest neighbor threshold technique" (discussed below), which informed us how to set the "operationalization" parameter for each factor input into the RTMDx Utility. This parameter assesses how each risk factor's spatial influence will be operationalized to a map and empirically assessed, that is, as a function of proximity, density, or both. "Proximity" (that is, Euclidean distance) proposes that being within a certain distance of the factor features increases the likelihood of illegal behavior and, ultimately, crime event locations. "Density" proposes that risk is higher at places where the factor features are highly concentrated, which creates a unique context for illegal behavior and, ultimately, crime. The RTMDx Utility also allows for testing "both" proximity or density. This

TABLE I   NN Analysis Results and Corresponding Risk Factor Operationalizations

Risk Factor	Operationalization	Observed Distance	P-Value	Spatial Pattern
Bowling Alleys	Proximity	9413.31	0.00	Dispersed
Coffee Shops	Proximity	7714.59	0.16	Random
Convenience Stores	Proximity	3582.76	0.00	Clustered
Foreclosures	Both	1407.76	0.00	Clustered
Gas Stations	Proximity	5620.99	0.00	Clustered
Gas Stations w/ Conv. Stores	Proximity	5620.99	0.00	Clustered
Grocery Stores	Both	3529.14	0.00	Clustered
Healthcare Centers and Gyms	Both	2658.99	0.00	Clustered
Laundromats	Proximity	5249.39	0.00	Clustered
Parking Stations and Garages	Both	1409.50	0.00	Clustered
Pawnshops	Proximity	9829.24	0.12	Random
Sit-Down Restaurants	Both	712.15	0.00	Clustered
Take-Out Restaurants	Both	1050.71	0.00	Clustered
Sports Arenas	Proximity	8892.15	0.00	Dispersed
Variety Stores	Proximity	5613.57	0.02	Clustered
Banks	Both	2062.48	0.00	Clustered
Bars	Both	2021.51	0.00	Clustered
Drug Markets	Density	433.43	0.00	Clustered
Rental Halls	Proximity	8461.02	0.01	Dispersed
Hotels	Both	1954.71	0.00	Clustered
Libraries	Proximity	13014.40	0.00	Dispersed
Liquor Licensed Retailers	Both	771.97	0.00	Clustered
Packaged Liquor Stores	Both	1704.62	0.00	Clustered
Movie Theaters	Proximity	6949.93	0.09	Clustered
Nightclubs	Proximity	6097.92	0.99	Random
Parks	Proximity	234.13	0.00	Clustered
Weapon Offending Parolees and Probationers	Both	717.40	0.00	Clustered
Susp. Person w/ Weapon	Density	700.27	0.00	Clustered
Schools	Both	2588.98	0.00	Clustered
Strip Clubs	Proximity	19072.13	0.00	Dispersed

setting permits the Utility to empirically select the best operationalization. However, this doubles the number of variables to be tested and greatly increases the analytical run time (or personal effort, if done by hand). So, to purposefully make this parameter decision for each potential risk factor, we consulted the output from the Nearest Neighbor (NN) analysis tool in the GIS. Table I shows the results of the NN analysis and the corresponding "operationalization" parameter that we ultimately selected to test for each risk factor.

To Produce Table 1

First, a NN threshold was calculated as: NN Threshold = 2 * (Block Length * Number of Analysis Increments). With insights gained from Taylor's (1997) research on behavior settings, we decided not to evaluate spatial influences beyond 3 blocks for this case study. So, we multiplied the block length of 462 feet by 3, and then doubled it. The multiplier of 2 was selected arbitrarily, but was intended to allow for conservative decision making about what operationalization methods to consider (or not). That is, it helped to prevent further ambiguity should we ever be tempted to break the "rule" for observed NN distance values very close to this threshold. With the multiplier of 2, we were comfortably strict about what operationalization parameter to set for each factor. The NN threshold for this case study is 2,772.

Then, for each set of factor feature points: If the features were not significantly clustered or if the observed mean distance reported by the NN analysis was greater than the NN threshold, the operationalization was set to "proximity." If the points were significantly clustered and the observed mean distance was less than or equal to the NN threshold, "both" proximity and density was tested, allowing the model to empirically determine the best one, if any. There were, however, some exceptions to this general rule. Risk factor datasets that represented a fleeting phenomenon (that is, they occurred at a location but did not remain a permanent feature of the environment), such as drug arrests or calls-for-service, were tested as a function of "density." And because the RTMDx Utility currently supports only point features as inputs, some polygon shapefiles had to be converted to (representative) point features prior to being tested (for example, parks were typically polygons shapefiles and were converted to point features).[3] Given the method of conversion, these risk factors were tested as "proximity" only.

So, the "density" operationalization method was specified for "drug markets" because these areas are defined using drug arrest data. This type of incident data is "fleeting" in the sense that arrests happen at places but do not remain a physical feature of the landscape for a long duration. For this potential risk factor, the *concentration* of data points is the best articulation of the environmental context created by these events and, therefore, the only spatial influence that we want to operationalize for the purpose of defining associated risk at certain places. In other words, "drug markets" are defined by proxy of a high spatial concentration of drug arrests. So, "high density" of drug arrests is the quality of the environment that we are particularly interested in. We recommend that all similar types of data that have a "fleeting" nature (for example, calls-for-service and shots fired) be tested with only the "density" operationalization method.

The "proximity" operationalization method was specified for "libraries" because we know libraries to be generally distributed throughout the study area without clustering. To save (run) time, it is reasonable to only test "proximity" from libraries; "density" spatial influence is not likely to be a significant operationalization. We recommend that all similar types of data—with spatial patterns that do not cluster, or for which the identification of a "density" spatial influence would not be practically meaningful for strategy purposes—be tested with only the "proximity" operationalization method.

The "both proximity and density" operationalization method was specified for "packaged liquor stores" because we want to let the RTMDx Utility make an empirical determination as to what spatial influence, if any, these features pose on the locations of outcome events. Packaged liquor stores are physical structures of the landscape and are not "fleeting" like drug arrests. They also have the potential to be clustered in certain areas, and their clustering could pose different spatial risks than their individual proximities to places in the study area. So, we want to test both possibilities.

Ultimately, this process resulted in the production of 129 maps of spatial influence measured as a function of either Euclidean distance or kernel density for each potential risk factor, respectively.

GENERAL COMMENTARY FOR STEP 6

This process of operationalizing spatial influence, whether it is informed by the results of a NN Analysis or otherwise, can be done manually (that is, "by hand"). It is rather simple map-making with the aid of a GIS, though it can be quite tedious when working with lots of potential risk factors. That is why we used the RTMDx Utility. Detailed technical steps for manually operationalizing spatial influence in a GIS can be found in the *Risk Terrain Modeling Manual* (Caplan & Kennedy, 2010). As with step 5, be sure to consider the construct validity of how spatial influences are operationalized.

SELECT AND WEIGHT MODEL FACTORS (STEPS 7 AND 8)

Prior RTM publications have discussed two methods for deciding what factors to include in a risk terrain model. The ad hoc method is based on insights from various sources and expert knowledge of the study area. It allows for manual (that is, "by hand") risk terrain map production and is best used when outcome event data do not exist, when outcome events are underreported or too few for statistical testing, or if valid and reliable outcome event data are not available. So, the ad hoc method is appropriate for producing risk terrain models for risk assessments that are done prior to the emergence of chronic crime problem places (because there is no outcome event data for statistical testing). To return to the chapter 1 example of a sidewalk and bushes that are perceived to be risky on a college campus: an ad hoc risk terrain model might be created to identify where these risky conditions colocate, even if crime has not yet occurred or clustered to create noticeable problems. This RTM might be informed by student, faculty, or staff surveys of risk perceptions and commissioned by college administrators who want to preemptively identify vulnerable areas and intervene to mitigate risks before one or more crimes occur. A study of this nature was conducted at Rutgers University-Newark, with a smart-phone-based survey app, to collect perceived risks of crime at places throughout the campus. Risk terrain models were produced based on these data and insights accordingly.

The empirical method requires statistical tests of the place-based correlation of each likely and accessible risk factor on the outcome events. This justifies the use of only the most significantly correlated risk factors in the risk terrain model (from the "pool" of many options). This is the preferred method when outcome event data exist and can be used as input for statistical testing, as is most often the case, given the histories of crime problems in many jurisdictions throughout the United States. The RTMDx Utility facilitates the empirical method of risk terrain map production by diagnosing the spatial factors that create vulnerabilities to crime throughout a landscape, based on the spatial patterns of recent past exposures. The intent of empirical RTM is to use recent past crime incidents as proxy measures of locations where a certain type of criminal behavior is preferred. The statistical procedures of RTM (and the RTMDx Utility) diagnose the features that are commonly located at high-crime places. This diagnosis can be used to create a risk terrain model and map that articulate these places and to forecast places where new crimes are likely to emerge or cluster in the future, given certain similar qualities of space and offender preferences.

We used the RTMDx Utility to empirically select risk factors (that is, Step 7) for inclusion in a risk terrain model. The Utility performed this step by using the 129 maps of spatial influence, operationalized from the 30 aforementioned factors (that is, the independent variables) and robbery incidents from calendar year 2012 (that is, the dependent variable, counts per cell), to build an elastic net penalized regression model assuming a Poisson distribution of events (Heffner, 2013). Generating 129 variables presents potential problems with multiple comparisons, in that we may uncover spurious correlations simply due to the number of variables tested. To address this issue, the Utility uses cross-validation to build a penalized Poisson regression model. Penalized regression balances model fit with complexity by pushing variable coefficients toward zero. The optimal amount of coefficient penalization was selected via cross-validation (Arlot & Celisse, 2010). This process reduces the large set of variables to a smaller set of variables with nonzero coefficients. For instance, although the "grocery store" factor is originally represented by six different maps, each with a different operationalization of spatial influence (that is, distance up to one block, distance up to two blocks, . . . density with a bandwidth equal to three blocks, and so on), this process identified that being within 1 block from a grocery store is the optimal operationalization of spatial influence for this factor. So, it kept this risk map layer and excluded others from further consideration. All resulting variables from this process play a useful ("significant") part within the model. But, since the goal is to build an easy-to-understand representation of spatial crime risk, the Utility further simplifies the model in subsequent steps via a bidirectional stepwise regression process.

It does this starting with a null model with no model factors, and measures the Bayesian Information Criteria (BIC) score for the null model. Then, it adds each model factor to the null model, and remeasures the BIC score. Every time the BIC score is calculated, the model with the best (lowest) BIC score is selected as the new candidate model (the model to surpass). The Utility repeats the process, adding and removing variables one step at a time until no factor addition or removal surpasses the previous BIC score. The Utility repeats this process with two stepwise regression models: one model assumes a Poisson and the other one assumes a negative binomial distribution. At the end, the RTMDx Utility chooses the factors that yield the best risk terrain model with the lowest BIC score between Poisson and negative binomial distributions. The Utility also produces a relative risk value (RRV) for comparison of the risk factors. RRVs for each risk factor presented in the output table are the exponentiated coefficients from the regression analysis (Heffner, 2013). Factor coefficients and RRVs can be interpreted as the weights of risk factors (which is step 8). In sum, the RTMDx Utility offers a statistically valid way to select and weight model factors for a risk terrain model that articulates risky places according to the spatial influences of features of a landscape.

GENERAL COMMENTARY FOR STEPS 7 AND 8

This process of selecting and weighting model factors, whether it is informed by the results of statistical testing or via the ad hoc method, can be done manually.[4] The technique discussed above, with cross-validation, regression modeling, and comparisons of BIC scores, is difficult to do by hand. However, it is possible for those who are statistically inclined. In fact, the RTMDx Utility performs all statistical tests in R, a free, open-source software environment for statistical computing and graphics (see www.r-project.org). Detailed steps for how the RTMDx Utility performs statistical tests and works with R can be found in the *RTMDx Utility User Manual* (Caplan, Kennedy, & Piza, 2013b).

When attempting to select and weight model factors, there are many reasonable ways to operationalize spatial influences of potential risk factors and then to test their place-based correlations with crime incident data. We encourage efforts to advance current "empirical" methods of RTM. At the core of any procedure, however, should be to operationalize the spatial influences of risk factors to a common geography and then to select only the most meaningful and valid factors for weighting and producing the final risk terrain model.

In 2012, there were 1,638 robberies in Kansas City, Missouri. The factors that spatially correlate with these crime incidents are presented in table 2, along with their most meaningful operationalization, spatial influential distance, and relative risk value. Table 2 demonstrates that, of the pool of 30 possible risk factors, only 14 are spatially related to robbery

TABLE 2   Risk Terrain Model Specifications

Risk Factor	Operationalization	Spatial Influence	Coefficient	Relative Risk Value
Nightclubs	Proximity	462	1.46	4.31
Weapon Offending Parolees and Probationers	Proximity	1386	1.45	4.28
Variety Stores	Proximity	462	1.08	2.95
Suspicious Person w/ Weapon	Density	1386	1.04	2.83
Grocery Stores	Proximity	462	0.89	2.44
Drug Markets	Density	924	0.89	2.29
Convenience Stores	Proximity	462	0.80	2.23
Packaged Liquor Stores	Proximity	924	0.66	1.93
Take-Out Restaurants	Proximity	924	0.46	1.58
Sit-Down Restaurants	Proximity	1386	0.46	1.58
Hotels	Density	1386	0.45	1.56
Banks	Density	1386	0.31	1.36
Schools	Proximity	1386	0.28	1.32
Foreclosures	Proximity	1386	0.20	1.23
Intercept	–	–	−4.97	–
Intercept	–	–	−0.75	–

incidents in this city: nightclubs, weapon offending parolees and probationers, variety stores, suspicious persons with a weapon, grocery stores, drug markets, convenience stores, packaged liquor stores, take-out restaurants, sit-down restaurants, hotels, banks, schools, and foreclosures. The RRVs can be interpreted as the weights of risk factors and may be easily compared. For instance, a place influenced by nightclubs has an expected rate of crime that is nearly three times higher than a place influenced by foreclosures (RRVs: 4.31 / 1.23 = 3.50). The most important predictor of robbery occurrence is proximity to nightclubs. Accordingly, all places may pose a risk of robbery to people in Kansas City, but because of the spatial influence of certain features of the landscape, some places are riskier than others.

COMBINE MODEL FACTORS (STEP 9)

RTM asserts that a place where the spatial influences of more than one of the model factors in table 2 colocate poses higher risks. This is articulated by combining risk map layers of the 14 factors in the final model using map algebra (Tomlin, 1994) and a GIS to produce a weighted risk terrain model. Based on the selected model factors and their coefficient values (that is, weights), a risk terrain model was produced using the following formula:

Exp(−4.9679 + 1.4602 * "Nightclubs" + 1.4545 * "Weapon Offending Parolees and Probationers" + 1.0812 * " Variety Stores" + 1.0412 * "Suspicious Person w/ Weapon" + 0.8939 * "Grocery Stores" + 0.8293 * "Drug Markets" + 0.8021 * "Convenience Stores" + 0.6582 * "Packaged Liquor Stores" + 0.4605 * "Take Out Restaurants" + 0.4588 * "Sit Down Restaurants" + 0.4456 * "Hotels" + 0.3080 * "Banks" + 0.2758 * "Schools" + 0.2035 * " Foreclosure") / Exp(−4.9679)

Raster cells continue to be the unit of analysis. So, based on the statistical techniques used above, the product of this formula is a "prediction" value for each cell that represents the expected count of outcome events in the cells for the same time duration of the input data. For instance, if the model is based on using the last 12 months of crime data (for example, calendar year 2012), then prediction values represent the expectation of crime counts at each cell for the next 12 months (for example, calendar year 2013). The predicted value of each cell is divided by the smallest prediction value among cells to create a new "relative risk score" that is easier to interpret. This rescaling causes the relative risk scores to begin at 1 and to represent how many times riskier a cell is compared to the least risky cell. For example, a cell with a risk score of 10 is twice as risky as a cell with the score of 5. The factor coefficients and relative risk scores are continuous numbers with "real" zeros. Therefore, as we demonstrated in our Kansas City example above, you can use these values as variables in other statistical analyses, such as a control variable or covariate for "environmental context" in a regression model.

A risk terrain map can be produced in a GIS by operationalizing the spatial influences of risk factors using the "best" risk terrain model specifications (for an example, in this case study, see table 2). Risk factors based upon proximity should be set (for example, "reclassified" in ArcGIS) to 1 for cells within the distance threshold and 0 for cells elsewhere. For example, in the Kansas City study area with an average block length of 462 feet, a raster map of a risk factor with a spatial influence of 2 blocks should have all cells within 924 feet of the risky feature set to a value of "1" and all other cells set to "0." Risk factors based upon density should be set (for example, "reclassified") to 1 for cells two standard deviations above the mean value after applying a kernel density operation of the specified bandwidth, and set to 0 for other cells.

Combine all risk map layers of model factors produced in a GIS through map algebra to create a risk terrain map and to calculate relative risk scores. For example, using the ArcGIS "raster calculator" function, we can type the formula above to assign relative risk scores to each cell.

The RTMDx Utility produced a risk terrain map for us as presented in table 2. Relative risk scores (RRSs) for each cell in the risk terrain map range from 1 (for the lowest risk place) to 983 (for the highest risk place). The highest risk places have an expected rate of robbery that is 983 times higher than a cell with a value of 1. The mean risk score is 4.89, with a standard deviation of 18.02. The map in figure 2 shows locations that are two standard deviations above the mean RRS, symbolized in red; they are considered the

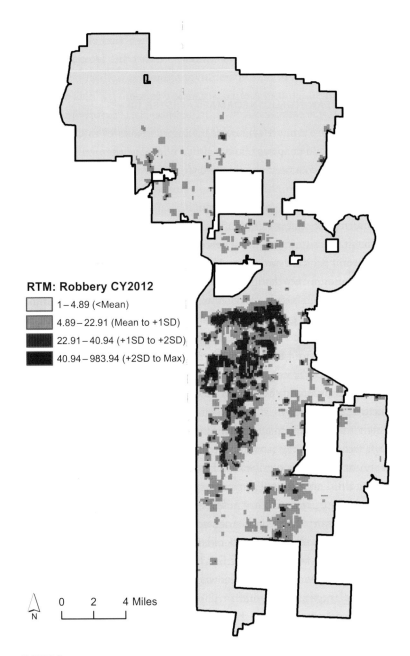

RTM: Robbery CY2012

- 1 – 4.89 (<Mean)
- 4.89 – 22.91 (Mean to +1SD)
- 22.91 – 40.94 (+1SD to +2SD)
- 40.94 – 983.94 (+2SD to Max)

0   2   4 Miles

N

FIGURE 2

Risk terrain map for Robbery in Kansas City, Missouri, 2012. As depicted, the likelihood of crimes occurring at some places is as much as 40 times greater than at other locations.

highest risk places for robbery in Kansas City. The likelihood of crimes occurring at these places is more than 40 times greater than at some other locations.

COMMUNICATE MEANINGFUL INFORMATION (STEP 10)

There are many ways to produce actionable intelligence from RTM. We will cover several different applications in chapters 6 and 7 of this book, and then we will discuss how to incorporate RTM and actionable intelligence into ACTION—a risk management agenda. For now, we just highlight two key sources of information derived from the RTM method: (1) tabular and (2) cartographic.

A lot of information and insights can be gleaned from table 2. It communicates not only what factors are significant attractors of robbery but also which ones are not particularly important (by their omission). This can inform decisions to stop paying attention to factors that were once thought to be important, such as parks, and focus attention on the spatial factors that truly correlate with the criminal behavior, but might have been overlooked, such as grocery stores. From this table, we also learn how model factors influence behavior and the extent of this influence. We might have assumed that bank locations relate to robbery incidents. But it appears that being within a certain distance from any bank is not the best operationalization of this factor's spatial influence. Rather, only areas with high concentrations of banks within three blocks attract robbery incidents and, therefore, have the greatest risk of this crime. Nightclubs might be given higher priority for intervention activities since they carry the greatest relative weight. But, according to the tabular output from RTM, we know to focus attention to within the immediate block of nightclub facilities, as opposed to farther away.

Comparing RRVs across model factors is useful for prioritizing risky features and for speculating why some features may pose exceptionally high risks compared to others, so that mitigation efforts can be implemented appropriately. For instance, drug markets may be high-risk due to the availability of large quantities of cash carried by buyers or dealers who would not seek assistance from the police. Foreclosures may be high-risk due to the absence of invested caretakers who would otherwise serve as "eyes and ears" within the area. Drug markets within 1,386 feet of a foreclosed property may present even greater risks. And so forth. If these mechanisms through which drug markets or foreclosures influence illegal behavior and pose risks of robbery are considered legitimate, then mitigation efforts can be developed and implemented accordingly. A similar problem-oriented process of risk mitigation can be had for each risk factor, with priority given to factors that have the highest RRVs. Once risk factors are identified, stakeholders can explore the (likely) mechanisms through which risks are presented and then initiate mitigation efforts. This is discussed more in chapters 7 and 8.

By viewing a risk terrain map in a GIS, we can adjust the symbology and design final map layouts to visually communicate the spatial vulnerabilities of a jurisdiction. Raster maps at the micro level, such as figure 2, can be created and presented as images in

TABLE 3   Negative Binomial Regression Results for 2012 Relative Risk Score on
2013 Robbery

Variable	IRR	Std. Err.	Z	95% C.I. Lower	95% C.I. Upper
Relative Risk Score (1–983.94)	1.054*	.00212	26.08	1.04984	1.05818

*p<0.001; Pseudo R2 = 0.1365; N=42803

reports or even prepared for layering in Google Earth. Rasters can be converted to vector and RRSs aggregated up via spatial joins to streets, police sectors, census tracts, cities, or regions. There are few limits as to the visual communication potential of risk terrain maps and related spatial data, far too many options to discuss here.

CRIME FORECASTING WITH RTM DIAGNOSES

Very accurate place-based forecasts can be made when the attractors of criminal behavior are diagnosed with RTM. Imagine an analyst in Kansas City producing a risk terrain model using data from the calendar year 2012, for the purpose of producing spatial intelligence that will inform decision making during calendar year 2013. The year goes by, and on January 1, 2014, the analyst wants to know how accurate her forecasts were for robbery. Using the 2012 RRSs as the independent variable and 2013 robbery incident locations as the dependent variable, she can conduct a test of the risk terrain model's predictive validity. As shown in table 3, the Incidence-Rate Ratio (IRR) from a negative binomial regression suggests that the calendar year 2013 robbery count increases 5.4% for every unit increase of RRSs at a 462ft place (that is, a cell approximately the size of a street block).[5] The range, mean, and standard deviation of RRSs are 1–983.94, 5.5, and 18.4, respectively. So, a cell with a RRS above the mean has at least a 30% increased likelihood of experiencing robberies (5.4 * 5.5). Places with risk scores one standard deviation above the mean have at least a 129% increased likelihood of experiencing robbery (5.4 * [5.5 + 18.4]). Places in the top 5% of high risk (that is, 2 standard deviations above the mean) have a 228% increased likelihood of experiencing robbery (5.4 * 42.3). These probabilities are statistically significant, so the risk terrain model produced a very accurate forecast of vulnerable places for robbery throughout Kansas City.

Places with high relative risk scores are behavior settings that present exceptionally strong likelihoods of robbery at these locations. However, there are many other factors that could be taken into account to assess spatial risks of robbery, such as temporal dynamics or recent past exposures; these will be discussed in detail in the coming chapters. Within the scope of this chapter, it can be said with statistical confidence that robbery incidents occur at places with particular features of the environment that present higher spatial risks.

There currently exist many methods to forecast crime locations. Some are arguably better than others. With any effort to forecast crime locations, a *successful* forecast should be clearly defined. What, then, are the requirements of a successful forecast? We consider the following to be the minimum requirements. First, the data used in the analysis should be reliable and valid, including both content and construct validities. The datasets and their sources should allow for replication and continued forecasting. This includes, but is not limited to, the requirement that the forecast technique does not rely heavily on the outcome of interest (that is, the dependent variable) to be the predictor, that is, the independent variable. Such a forecasting technique would not be sustainable if it were considered to be actionable *and* successful since outcomes would ultimately be prevented.

This brings us to the second requirement, that the outputs of the forecast should be operational. That is, it should be reasonably clear what to do with the information, either to respond to the forecasted effects or to modify the inputs to create a different forecast. Third, the method of the forecast should be operationalized consistently from one instance to another. Datasets and sources may change, as will analysts and other factors, but the reliability of the forecasting method must withstand multiple iterations, in different settings, by different people, and for different types of outcome events. Fourth, the elements of the forecast should be articulable, with the importance of each factor relative to one another directly measured. The direct impact of key factors on outcomes should be demonstrable (that is, have internal validity). Fifth, the output results should be within a range of reasonable expectations (that is, have face validity). If the forecast suggests something that is unlikely to occur according to past experience or theoretical knowledge, the forecasting process should be able to justify why that result was produced or else the forecasting process should be able to be revised in a nonarbitrary way.

When comparing various hot spot forecasting techniques, different studies have come to contradictory conclusions (see Chainey, Tompson, & Uhlig, 2008; Dugato, 2013; Hart & Zandbergen, 2012, 2013; Van Patten, McKeldin-Coner, & Cox, 2009). To overcome this ambiguity, Chainey et al. (2008) proposed the metric measure of the Predictive Accuracy Index (PAI) to assess the accuracy of hot spot techniques at predicting future crime locations. The PAI examines the hit rate in relation to the hot spot area and overall study area. While the PAI measures accuracy, it is still possible to be accurate without being precise. The Recapture Rate Index (RRI) compares the rate of change from one time period to the predicted time period and complements the PAI measure. Precision and accuracy of a forecast are important considerations for defining success. Drawve (2014), Drawve, Moak, & Berthelot (2014), Dugato (2013), and others have independently demonstrated the precision and accuracy of RTM methods. However, the problem with a focus on only precision or accuracy of forecasts is that reliability can be suspect under certain circumstances. For example, if crime *never* moves, then past crime incidents will always be 100% accurate and precise predictors of new incident locations. Alternatively, if crime *always* moves, then new crimes will never occur where past crimes did, making this event-dependent forecasting technique 0% accurate and precise. The reality of crime patterns is likely somewhere in between these extremes. But regardless, such a forecasting method would not be considered successful, in and of itself, according to our aforementioned minimum requirements because the outputs of the forecast must also be operational. If police were to intervene successfully in response to the forecast and their actions changed the spatial dynamics of crime, then the forecast could be very accurate or precise prior to the intervention and then not at all accurate or precise after the intervention. Basically, any successful forecast should yield valuable information that can be operationalized for preventative action. However, if the action is successful at reducing crime incident counts or changing their spatial patterns, then it could directly and deleteriously affect the precision or accuracy of future forecast iterations. Sixth and finally, then, a successful forecast technique should be able to tolerate the products of successful interventions, especially those that are based on the intel from prior forecast iterations.

3

CRIME EMERGENCE, PERSISTENCE, AND EXPOSURE

Since we consider that crime is more likely to occur in places that have high risk according to the calculation of a risk terrain model, it should also be evident that for crime to start, something about the place creates the conditions that are ripe for its emergence. This observation is not a surprise to anyone who understands cities. Efforts that are made to improve some areas have had the effect of reducing crime. But, equally, when areas are left to decline, it is evident that crime often accompanies physical disorder. This underscores the view we expressed concerning the importance of the environmental context in creating conditions for crime to occur. But spatial risk is not an absolute. So, spatial risk assessment must consider not only the conventional aspects of environmental characteristics determined by the presence of facilities, such as nightclubs, that might attract crime. It is also important to remember that these nightclubs are frequented by people who provide good targets for victimization and that their presence attracts offenders to these locations. An example of this is found in our recent work with The World Bank, when we found there to be a high risk of robbery or mugging presented by nightclubs in the tourist district of Bogotá, Columbia, but less so elsewhere in the city. Tourists seeking to experience the nightlife are "good targets" and areas near nightclubs are attractive locations for offending behavior directed at these targets.

This metric is not terribly hard to grasp intuitively, but it has been historically challenging to operationalize in criminological research. Part of the reason for this has been the difficulties researchers have had in simultaneously considering the situational risk factors of crime and spatial vulnerability. In addition, the coincident effects of the occurrence of large amounts of crime repeatedly in certain areas have provided a distraction for analysts and law enforcement in their attempts to identify and target criminogenic places. As clusters of crime, or hot spots, point to where problems concentrate, it appears logical that police would go there to solve the problem. But, as we explain in chapter 4, police presence in these areas is itself a factor in aggravating or mitigating the spatial risk of crime at the targeted areas and throughout the rest of the jurisdiction. Police successes in dealing with people at hot spots may have the effect of deterring criminals or even reducing crime counts at these areas. But, despite this, the underlying spatial factors that attract and generate problems in these areas do not go away. So, three things can happen: crime disappears, it moves, or it subsides, to reappear at a later date. Police describe to us the feeling of playing Whack-a-Mole with crime. They will often focus on hot spot areas only to have crime emerge elsewhere and then return to the original location once police leave.

The emergence of crime relates to issues raised by the extent and concentration of spatial influences, where the spatial context of the landscape is likely to increase potential for new crime incidents. In the RTM framework, we take a step that is basic to the development of GIS in assuming that certain places can acquire attributes that, when combined in prescribed ways, define contexts in which certain outcomes are made more probable. So, as an example, the attributes of places that have many people moving through them in the evening or late at night, combined with the presence of many liquor-dispensing establishments, nearby parking lots, and so on, may denote an area that is perceived as an entertainment district that is fun for people to go to for social events. These attributes combined can be used to predict the types of behavior that we would expect in this area, reducing the likelihood that our predictions about what would transpire there are wrong. In this way, then, we use attributes of places to assign the risk that certain things will happen in a particular geography. Now, these outcomes may be benevolent (for example, people meeting up with friends and enjoying a night out) or they may take on a more sinister character where a combination of certain types of factors creates a context in which the risk of negative outcomes (including crime) increases.

Let's step away from crime for just a moment with an analogy in a different and much more benign context. Consider a place where children play repeatedly. When we step back from our focus on the cluster of children, we might realize that located where they play are swings, slides, and open fields. These features of the place (that is, suggestive of a playground) attract children and playful behavior there instead of other locations that do not have such entertaining qualities. In a similar but more menacing way, spatial factors can influence the seriousness and longevity of crime problems. The ability to use RTM to identify, or diagnose, spatial factors that enhance crime risk is useful for anticipating future crime incident locations and preemptively addressing the criminogenic qualities of these places. RTM is not sufficient in offering a complete picture of whether or not a crime will definitely occur in a location, despite it being a high-risk place. In considering spatial intelligence, it is also necessary to integrate the benefits of knowing which areas have been historically exposed to high levels of crime incidents. Knowledge of such areas also influences how or when people choose to use them. So, the history of an area can affect the criminal behavior presently located there.

Returning to the example of a place characterized by features of a playground, these attributes may be used to forecast certain types of behaviors and events located there. But the attributes themselves do not create the playful outcomes; they simply point to locations where, if the conditions are right, the likelihood of experiencing them will be high. So, toddlers will frequent playgrounds that are perceived by parents to be more age-appropriate for younger children. Parents or toddlers who develop a personal liking to one particular playground will frequent it more often and may even encourage other toddlers' parents to give it a try. Inevitably, some playgrounds will become more popular than others, resulting in repeated use by many children. Thus, the place becomes a persistent "hot spot" of playful activity.

The emergence of playful activity in this place is predictable, given the spatial influences of nearby (playground) features. Its recent past exposures to children playing (that is, its history) also increase the likelihood that new playful activities will continue, unless something drastic happens to this place. In a recent case in a New Jersey shore town, many children enjoyed a public beachfront playground, with equipment made of metal. The place was ideal for young children to play, yielding regular patterns of activity year round. But unfortunately, the salty-air quickly rusted and weakened the metal, creating unsafe conditions. As word spread about the hazardous equipment, fewer parents brought their children over time. The city responded by removing the metal equipment and replacing it with new materials. Children returned in short order.

The concept of *exposure* considers peoples' histories and "collective memories" of places, and helps us to further define crime risk as a spatial-temporal function of previous crime events. Cartographically modeling spatial vulnerability as the clustering of spatial influences of criminogenic features and then interpreting vulnerability in the context of exposure permit a research strategy to identify and manage these risky places. Crime risks, then, are both spatial and situational, affected by exposure to individual crime incidents that appear from location to location, by exposure to places where crime persists and clusters over time, and by the spatial influences of one or more criminogenic features of the landscape.

In our study of violent crimes in Irvington, New Jersey (Caplan, Kennedy, & Piza, 2013a), we found that (the calendar year) 2007 violent crime incident locations were a significant predictor of 2008 violent crime incident locations. This finding is consistent with the premise of hot spot mapping and its related empirical research (for example, Chainey et al., 2008; Gorr & Olligschlaeger, 2002). But including a measure of spatial vulnerability yielded an even better model of future violent crime locations compared to predictions made with past violent crime incidents alone. The regression model, inclusive of both past violent crime counts and relative risk scores derived from RTM, explained more than twice the variance. Places in Irvington with higher risk scores had a 458% increased likelihood of future violent crimes compared to places with lower risk scores, when controlling for the presence of prior violent crime incidents. These results, and subsequent similar findings from studies of different crime types in a variety of other settings, led us to generally conclude that crimes occur at places with greater spatial vulnerabilities, especially if similar crimes occurred there already, and that they persist for as long as *both* of these factors remain unchanged.

Through the operationalization of spatial influences of criminogenic features in a GIS, we can infer which places are likely to attract illegal behavior and, therefore, have the highest relative risks of crime. When offenders occupy these spaces and commit crimes, these events establish the "crime history" of a place, which could encourage additional motivated offenders to commit similar crimes. A place's exposure to offenders and crimes brings about additional characteristics that might threaten others and alter newer perceptions of the place (and also attract attention from law enforcement). This leads us to conclude that the emergence, persistence, and desistance of crime are dynamically linked to these factors of vulnerability and exposure. We will return to this in chapter 4.

SPATIAL-TEMPORAL VULNERABILITY OF CRIME

While it is true that vulnerability to crime varies across space, it is also true that the same places can have varying risk levels depending on the time of day or day of week, despite the stationary nature of landscape features. This is because spatial influences of environmental features are dynamic and can change accordingly. Grubesic and Mack (2008) have argued that we cannot treat space and time as independent entities; rather, we must treat them as interdependent ones that interact to create situational risks. Andresen and Malleson (2011) have looked at this issue and developed means by which to create more accurate assessments of crime risk, taking into account population movements. Temporal variations in opportunity and ambient populations are important for calculations that we make in evaluating overall risk. The interactions among people and their geographies are deeply fluid in the sense that no feature retains its "social relevancy" permanently (Kinney, 2010, p. 485). Places can be "fantastically dynamic places" (Jacobs, 1961/1992, p. 14). For instance, the spatial influence of a bar at 10 PM on a Friday is intuitively going to be different than its spatial influence at 10 AM on a Tuesday. Basically, places can have different risks at different times because a criminogenic feature can have varying spatial influences depending on its social relevancy at different times and under particular circumstances.

In work that we completed with our colleagues Yasemin Irvin-Erickson[1] and Eric Piza, we studied the temporally dynamic influences of landscape features in Newark, New Jersey, on robbery incidents[2] acquired from the Newark Police Department (NPD) for the calendar year 2010. The address-level data were classified according to their date (that is, 07/28/2010), day (that is, Monday, Saturday), and hour (0 to 23, 0 denoting

12 AM) of occurrence. This study selectively focused on street robberies, which occurred in public places (that is, streets, sidewalks, parking lots, lots or yards, and in front of commercial dwellings). We looked at incidents occurring in places of 145ft by 145ft (N = 21,931) throughout the city. This place size was chosen because it represents half the approximate median length of a Newark city block (290 feet).

Risk terrain models for robberies at three different hour-groups were created: 6 AM to 6 PM (business hours), 6 PM to 2 AM (happy hours), and 2 AM to 6 AM (bedtime hours). In confirming the social relevancy link between these time periods and different activities, we examined the hours of operation of major facilities in Newark. For instance, during the weekday and weekend, the majority of the train and bus service inbound to and outbound from Newark starts at 5:30 to 6:00 AM and goes through 2:00 AM. The entertainment venues in Newark (that is, restaurants, bars, and the like) are open until 1:00 to 2:00 AM. When looking at the day of the week, we examined robberies that took place on weekdays and those that happened during the weekend.

We determined that the most important factor related to robberies in the calendar year (CY) risk terrain model was proximity to bus stops. It was also important for the CY 2010 weekday and weekend business and happy hour models. This factor was less important for the weekday and weekend bedtime hours. We speculated that this was due to the travel patterns of people to and from their residences (Lemieux & Felson, 2012).

Light rail stops exerted a criminogenic spatial influence on robberies during the weekday business hours, but lost this influence during weekday happy hours and bedtime hours and on the weekend. We speculated that transportation stops attract individuals during the weekday and are unlikely to be frequented at other times when service is light or nonexistent.

Schools had a criminogenic spatial influence on CY 2010 robberies and CY 2010 weekday business hour robberies; they lost this influence for the weekday happy hours and bedtime hours and for the weekend, when they are closed. In contrast, bars and take-out restaurants, which did not have a criminogenic influence during the daytime business hours, became criminogenic features after business hours, when these facilities are more likely to operate and be more heavily occupied. Other factors have similar temporal differences. Sit-down restaurants emerge as criminogenic features at late hours during the week and at early hours during the weekend. Bus stops and grocery stores, on the other hand, emerged as criminogenic features in almost all temporal risk terrain models, likely because people frequent them across all time periods. Pawnshops appeared important for robbery only during the happy hours on a weekend, while prostitution areas were criminogenic for robbery only during weekday bedtime hours. Drug markets were important during weekday business and happy hours and weekend happy hours, but were not important predictors of robbery during bedtime hours.

From this study (Gaziarifoglu, Kennedy, & Caplan, 2012; Irvin-Erickson, 2014), and subsequent work by Yerxa (2013), we can say that the spatial influence of criminogenic features is uniform neither across different temporal units nor in relation to one another.

According to the results of our studies, risk terrain maps that articulate these unique spatial-temporal vulnerabilities have, in some models, explained the variance in robbery incident locations by more than 50%. This is no small feat considering that Weisburd and Piquero (2008) have commented that most criminal justice research does not often explain variations in crime by more than 20%. This work illustrates the flexibility of the RTM approach, which allows not only an assessment of risk factors in certain places, but an ability to judge their effects at different times of the day and days of the week.

LOW RISK, COLD SPOTS

When we consider how crime emerges and persists, we need to think about not just those places that attract criminal behavior, but also those that do not. It is not always the case that risk levels will stay constantly high since some factors that we would consider (such as spatial influence, known offenders, or police activity) are dynamic and might move or change a fair amount. But it is reasonable to expect that most high-risk areas stay that way for some period of time. It is also evident from previous research that lower-risk areas, or cold spots, often surround high-risk areas. These are areas where crime occurrence tends to be relatively low.

Cold spots probably exist because of the absence of spatial influences of features that promote criminal behavior or the presence of factors whose spatial influences deter it—that is, protect against it (Kinney, Brantingham, Wuschke, Kirk, & Brantingham 2008). As Weisburd (2008) points out, it is unrealistic to assume that if we tackle crime problems in a supermarket through effective police intervention, this crime will appear on the next street if there is no supermarket. A distant supermarket might suffer the consequence of this intervention but it seems unlikely. Cold spots appear for reasons more than the lack of targets. The persistence of cold spots appears to relate to the low levels of spatial vulnerability identified in a risk terrain model. Or they may be areas in which there are protective factors that mitigate exposures, such as high levels of community involvement in prevention or proactive policing. If we look for examples of cold spots, we may point to such things as business districts that have private security or areas around schools or universities. The formal surveillance that these institutions provide is combined with the informal network of people using these areas that are aware of their security and expect protection. If these factors are present, the fact that cold spots remain cold and not conducive to criminal behavior over time further supports the idea that geography matters.

The sustained levels of low risk in some areas also support the notion that, even in high-crime areas, places can be made safe. An interesting example of this is found in the newly located sports and entertainment facilities that have been built in inner-city areas. While the areas around these complexes remain high-risk, the corridors into and out of these locations, as well as the venues themselves, appear to have maintained good records of safety for staff and customers alike (examples of these include inner-city facilities in Newark, Los Angeles, and Detroit). Cold spots can be maintained by police activity, but they are also a product of efforts to alter the environments in order to mitigate spatial risk.

Risk of crime is a consequence of the types of environments in which people live, work, play, or travel through. Risky places can be dynamic and are a function of both spatial vulnerabilities and exposures. Spatial vulnerability can be affected by the social relevancy of features of landscapes, which can vary by time of day or week. The analysis of these factors of vulnerability and exposure leads to actionable spatial intelligence. The next chapter examines the underlying principles related to crime exposure and the related topics of opportunity, crime hot spots, and near repeats. It seeks to explain how all of these factors might interact to create risky places for crime.

4

PRESENCE, REPEATS, AND CONCENTRATION: EXPOSURES TO CRIME

OPPORTUNITY AND CRIME

Spatial analysis using mapping techniques has become integrated into the day-to-day strategic and operational processes of police agencies around the United States and, increasingly, in countries throughout the world. The identification of crime hot spots through GIS mapping and the targeting of police activity to these places have been recognized in high-quality evaluation research as an effective crime-fighting technique (Braga, 2005; Braga, Papachristos, & Hureau, 2012). Yet despite the evident success of hot spot mapping, there is a manifest disconnect between the conventional practices of this spatial analysis and the responses by police agencies to address crime problems where crime incidents cluster. While hot spot mapping is spatial, or place-based (Weisburd, 2008), police responses to crime at these areas are often inherently offender-focused. That is, hot spot mapping tells police where to go using existing crime problems, but not what to do about the *places* when they get there. So, police often focus interventions on the people located within hot spot areas in an effort to alter the "routine activities" (Cohen & Felson, 1979) of offenders and reduce opportunities for crime.

In 1979, Cohen and Felson's routine activities theory explained that crime occurrence could be more easily facilitated if there are motivated offenders, suitable targets of victimization, and an absence of capable guardians. Affecting this "crime triangle" became the goal of many police agencies, that is, the goal was to be the "present capable guardians." A few years later, in 1981, Cohen, Kluegel, and Land refashioned the routine activities theory, renaming it "opportunity" theory, to include concepts of exposure, proximity, guardianship, and target attractiveness as variables that increase the risk of victimization. Opportunity theory explained that the convergence of these factors leads to the conditions in which crime will occur. Police were further pressured (and felt the need) to be the "capable guardians" in the right places at the right times.

Throughout the 1980s, spatial analysis of crime gained prominence in the research community when criminologists began to study the distribution of crime incidents at places. One of the seminal works was published by Sherman, Gartin, and Buerger in 1989. They found that 3% of all the calls-for-service addresses in Minneapolis accounted for 50% of the crime incident locations. Similar findings that crime incidents cluster have been made by many other researchers across numerous jurisdictions. Armed with these insights and newly available GIS technologies, early spatial analysis techniques enabled geographic allocations of police officers to more strategically disrupt opportunities for crime.

Today it is common knowledge that crime incidents do not distribute uniformly or randomly across places, or "small micro units of analysis" (Weisburd, 2008, p. 2): they cluster. So, the analytical approach selected to study and forecast crime patterns plays a critical role in the reliability and validity of efforts to assess vulnerabilities and future crime hot spots. Eck (2001, 2002), Lee and Alshalan (2005), Mears, Scott, and Bhati (2007), Basta, Richmond, and Wiebe (2010), Groff, Weisburd, and Yang (2010), and Brantingham and Brantingham (1995) all directly state or imply the spatial nature of criminogenic opportunities. Theorists such as Cohen, Felson, and others (for example, Cohen et al., 1981; Simon, 1975) have suggested that spatial variations in crime are explained by opportunities to commit crime at locations that are accessible to the offender, and have argued that "the risk of criminal victimization varies dramatically among the circumstances and locations in which people place themselves and their property" (Cohen & Felson, 1979, p. 595). Crime analysis and prevention activities, Cohen et al. (1981) argued, should consider not only who is involved in the criminal events, but also the environmental characteristics of where crimes occur and cluster. A common thread among opportunity theorists and related scholarly thinkers is that the unit of analysis for "opportunity" is a place, and that the dynamic nature of that place constitutes opportunities for crime.

Problematic for opportunity theorists is the fact that they generally only have had data that depict large areas and, so, have been unable to test microlevel effects of environmental characteristics on crime. Andresen (2014) says that opportunity theory is scalable but it really is a macro theory evoked in microlevel analysis. In these instances, the approach generally has been an attempt to test victimization for certain groups in distinct environments. Spatial analysis is not often informed by opportunity theories except indirectly because, as Andresen (2014) reports, it is difficult to operationalize these activities in an ever-changing environment using aggregate data.

Opportunity crimes are difficult to forecast using the characteristics of the actors involved, especially when forecasts rely on past incidents for measures of the likelihood of new crime events happening. We very rarely have clear measures of the prior status of people (that is, offenders or victims) that we can use to preemptively identify them. Even in the case where we can pinpoint potential offenders by their past crimes, the link to their routine activities that create opportunities is loose. So, too, are the bases upon which they make their choices. While we could agree that these choices occur to maximize benefits to the offender, it is not clear where and under what circumstances these choices are made, except after the fact. And, arguably, they are not always "rational" from an outsider's perspective (Cornish & Clarke, 1986). This is not to say that research is nonexistent on individual choices, but the research has not been done on an aggregated micro-level basis (Miethe, Stafford, & Long, 1987; Osgood, Wilson, O'Malley, Bachman, & Johnston, 1996). Nor does it argue that an analytical approach that focuses on past crime incidents to predict future crime incidence has no value. On the contrary, a key component in crime forecasting is the development of strong measures of past events to add to our calculation of the future likelihood of crime. But, to understand how this would occur, we need to delve more deeply into what constitutes viable measures of past events. In the next few pages, we consider this in the context of exposure to crime. We examine crime incidents as measures of something more than merely fleeting events on a landscape. They are symptoms of other phenomena at places throughout the landscape. They are the outcomes of individual choices, patterns of which we can study for a better understanding of why people choose certain areas to commit crime and not others.

Let us start with the premise, as do routine activity theorists, that the presence of victims and offenders will lead to crime, particularly if there is no one in authority who can stop it from happening. The mechanisms for this crime to occur are not clear except that the offender is motivated and the victim is vulnerable. This is a good starting point in trying to understand crime and has been a meaningful focus for crime analysts. But it brings up a few questions: Does this copresence always result in crime? No. In addition, are there characteristics of the offenders, victims, or situations that make crime more likely in this moment than at other times? Most likely; however, the research that has looked at these issues measured presence of actors and assessed consequences after the fact and, thus, is restricted in its abilities to specify the actual dynamics that occur in setting the conditions for crime.

Now, imagine that we want to improve on this analysis by examining how likely a crime is to occur in a place if crime occurred there before. We assume presence of offenders and victims as stable and aim to seek how likely a "near repeat" is to happen. This analysis addresses contagion of crime, and its implicit assumption is that recent past crime occurrence is a signal to motivated offenders that this place is good for the commission of new crimes. Again, the mechanisms for promoting near repeats are not all that clear, although there is some suggestion that they occur through a series of choices that offenders make. This seems reasonable, given that it makes sense to assume that offenders are trying to maximize their gain while reducing their costs (that is, the risk of getting caught). So, if other offenders were successful, had significant gains, and so on, then they might too. Again, though, the connection between the actual choice mechanisms and the measurement of near repeats is not fully explicated. When many near repeat crimes occur at an area, clusters form. Studying crime clusters, or hot spot mapping, is a way of examining crime occurrence, that is, looking at crime incidents in terms of spatial concentration.

In the next section, we will further discuss these two types of exposures to crime: hot spots and near repeats. For now, the takeaway point is that the occurrence of crime supports the idea that the key actors have converged as predicted by opportunity theory. The crime incidents that occur in one place will create conditions for further crimes. The crimes that occur in these places close to one another must be somehow linked to one another beyond their common geography. In practical terms, then, the operationalization of each of these statements based on opportunity theory, near repeat analysis, or hot spot mapping is crime dependent, with our assessments of where crime takes place, why it happens, and what to do about it focused on the incidents themselves and the people directly associated with them. An advantage of these approaches includes the increased attention paid by police to certain areas and, perhaps, an evidenced-based strategy for crime containment. This has been most clearly demonstrated with the integration of CompStat meetings into the regular operations of many police departments, though we will turn to a cautionary tale of Comp-Stat in chapter 8. The disadvantage of this event-dependent approach is that we are left with limited understanding of why crimes occur in the first place (emergence) and, if they disappear, where the next crime or hot spot is likely to emerge.

It would be foolish to dismiss the importance of past crime incidents in encouraging future crime problems. Obviously, a clustering of crime in a certain place signifies that there is something going on in that location that is conducive to crime. The crime cluster is a symptom of some other phenomena at this place. Using only crime incident data, however, we are unable to establish the exact mechanisms for why this symptom appears. Crime occurring in the same place over time may simply be a function of what the Brantinghams have called the stationarity fallacy, which emphasizes the fact that hot spot maps often display combinations of unrelated incidents that happen over time and are plotted as though they are somehow connected beyond sharing a common geography (Brantingham & Brantingham, 1981). Thinking of individual crime incidents or hot spots as signs and symptoms of underlying risks at places permits further inquiry into the spatial characteristics of these places. The spatial influences of certain environmental features at these places could be affecting and enabling the seriousness and longevity of crime problems. Returning to an earlier example, a sole focus on hot spots is like observing that children frequently play at the same place every day and then calling that place a hot spot for children playing, but without acknowledging the presence of swings, slides, and open fields. Hot spots of crime, then, serve more as a proxy measure of places where the dynamic interactions of underlying criminogenic factors exist or persist over time.

To broaden our approach to crime analysis in an effort to overcome the limitations of event-based inquiries, we need to understand the specifics of how researchers have studied crime concentration and contagion to date. These approaches can be best summarized as focusing on exposure, either from individual crime incidents, from a contagion effect from the fact that a crime incident occurred nearby, or from a concentration effect that is based on the fact that new crime incidents cluster around older crime incident locations. Let's look in detail at how these have been studied in the literature. Then we will consider these forms of exposures in the context of spatial vulnerability.

EXPOSURE TO CRIME

HOT SPOTS

Exposure turns attention to the targets of crime and their relationship to offenders and their surroundings. For victims, how do they judge their risk of harm in certain places and what steps do they take to reduce this risk? Is it the case that crime victims simply miscalculate the risks they are taking, resigned to the dangers that lurk in the areas that they frequent? Or, more likely, do they take steps that allow them to be crime-free most of the time, understanding that the environments they inhabit combine with their risk profile to increase the likelihood of victimization?

Since crimes cluster spatially (Weisburd, 2008; Weisburd & Braga, 2006; Sherman et al., 1989; Sherman, 1995), crime prevention resources "should be similarly concentrated rather than diffused across urban areas" to achieve maximum impact (Braga & Weisburd, 2010, p. 34). This ideal has become well established in law enforcement, with contemporary police agencies directing resources to high-crime places (Weisburd, 2008). Geographically focused police practices have consistently demonstrated measured effectiveness. A meta-analysis by Braga, Papachristos, and Hureau (2012) identified nine studies of hot spot policing efforts with sufficiently rigorous designs, seven of which reported noteworthy crime reductions. In the case of the Minneapolis RECAP program (Sherman et al., 1989), the lack of a reduction was attributed to the fact that too many addresses were assigned to the program, making officers unable to provide significant coverage to enough high-crime places. Recent randomized controlled designs provide additional support for place-based policing efforts. Initiatives in Jacksonville, Florida (Taylor, Koper, & Woods, 2011), Lowell, Massachusetts (Braga & Bond, 2008), and Philadelphia, Pennsylvania (Ratcliffe, Taniguchi, Groff, & Wood, 2011), generated significant crime reductions by focusing police efforts to high-crime places.

Place-based interventions can also offer a more efficient method of policing than offender-based strategies. While places often demonstrate relatively stable crime levels over time, it is well established that individuals experience both short-term and long-term variations in criminal propensity. Weisburd (2008, p. 6), for example, noted that police in Seattle would have to target four times as many people as places to account for 50% of the crime incidents between 1989 and 2002. Of particular interest to contemporary criminal justice researchers and crime analysts are the patterns of concentration that appear with criminal events (Sherman et al., 1989; Braga & Weisburd, 2012). Hot spot maps have, then, led to more geographically focused and strategic allocations of police resources to combat crime problems.

Crime incidents can create an event-dependent effect, either because of the changes that occur in response to crime forming hot spots or because of the contagion effect of repeat criminal behavior. Researchers have studied the concentration of crime incidents that appear as hot spots and the changes that take place over time in these areas (Weisburd, 2008; Weisburd & Braga, 2006; Sherman et al., 1989; Harries, 1999; Ratcliffe, 2006). Ongoing studies of specific hot spot areas have highlighted conditions that contribute to their appearance and persistence (Mazerolle, Kadleck, & Roehl, 1998). In addition, researchers have looked at the general appearance of crime across areas, with increased attention paid to the role that certain underlying decision processes, spurred either by police intervention or by offender choices, play in creating patterns of crime that can be detected, monitored, and controlled over time (Groff & La Vigne, 2002).

Short, Brantingham, Bertozzi, and Tita (2010) simulated hot spots using assumptions about the relative importance of victims, offenders, and guardians in influencing the emergence and movement of hot spots throughout an urban landscape. They found, in their analysis, that efforts to suppress supercritical hot spots result in only a temporary disruption of crime patterns. The authors suggest that their model demonstrates that new hot spots appear even after police actions are simulated. They go on to say, "Moreover, simulations show clearly that suppression over the central area of a crime hot spot drives the elevated risk into a ring surrounding the area of suppression, corresponding to the ring solution in our nonlinear analysis. The displaced hot ring then breaks up to form independent hot spots of the stable bump solution in the nonsymmetric case" (p. 3964). The reverse finding appears for what they refer to as subcritical crime hot spots. These do not displace, nor do they reemerge.

The authors were somewhat surprised by these findings since, at least in the case of supercritical hot spots, they run counter to the empirical studies that suggest that crime will not displace when suppressed through prevention acts of law enforcement (Guerette & Bowers, 2009). The authors explored reasons for why their simulation would run counter to the evidence. They state that one reason for this finding might be their assumption in the model that the environmental landscapes they are studying are homogeneous. The reason for the lack of empirical observation of displacement in empirical settings is that "environments are sufficiently heterogeneous to limit the feasibility of offenders moving from favored habitats to adjacent areas that may be bereft of targets or victims, or may experience much higher levels of surveillance" (p. 3965). Hot spot displacement in the model may also be due, they suggest, to the fact that investigations have not looked far enough away from the area of suppression to detect reemergence elsewhere.

The findings in the Short et al. study are intriguing because they point to a problem that exists in the conceptual structure of hot spot analysis. Attention is focused on the crime incident itself as a measure of the hot spot. In their study, the relationships of offenders, victims, and guardians were explored in relation to crime. But crime events do not occur out of spatial context, as reasoned in the explanation for contrary findings in the Short et al. paper. Displacement, they suggest, could relate to opportunity or risk nearby. But risk is not defined solely by the crime occurrence or the colocation of offenders. Risk is also contextual and can be a function of the character of the environment in which these offenders, victims, and guardians operate. So, the emergence of crime hot spots outside of suppressed areas may not have to do solely with the homogeneous nature of their simulated environment but can be affected by the environment itself.

In a paper from 2010, Ratcliffe explores the problem of crime dispersion and emergence. He discusses the fact that we have not developed sufficiently good tools to identify how crime moves around despite efforts at such assessments like near repeat analysis, which provides a framework for looking at the serial nature of crime occurrence. In dealing with the question of dispersal, Ratcliffe suggests a test that would allow us to identify where crime is likely to locate using previous clusters. This analysis uses a dispersal technique that improves upon, by Ratcliffe's calculation, previous attempts at studying crime movement through the use of Location Quotients. In looking at this work, it is still evident that the calculation for dispersal of crime remains dependent solely on the previous occurrence of crime. Reboussin, Warren, and Hazelwood (1995) describe a map that displays the spatial orientation of only a single phenomenon (for example, crime) as a "mapless map." As explained by Rengert and Lockwood (2009), "A mapless map is a mere description since it describes how one variable is distributed in space; whether it clustered or uniformly distributed for example. In order to determine 'why' it is distributed the way it is, the spatial distribution of at least one other variable needs to be considered" (p. 109). So, in considering Ratcliffe's dispersion analysis in the context of the findings by Short et al. related to displacement, it seems that a technique that takes into account both previous crime occurrence and spatial context would improve upon prior analyses and address the problem of the "stationarity fallacy" that plagues all hot spot analysis. Crime incidents (clustered or not) do, however, occur sequentially in time. So, next, we consider the contagion effects of crime incidents.

NEAR REPEATS

Near repeat, or contagion, models assume that if a crime occurs at a location, the chances of a new future crime occurring nearby increases for a particular period of time (Ratcliffe & Rengert, 2008; Bowers & Johnson, 2005; Johnson, 2008). If victims misjudge or are unable to control their exposure, their risk of crime under certain conditions such as this goes up. This type of exposure may lead to serial victimization as well, which suggests that individuals are unable to control either their vulnerability or their exposure and are revictimized as a consequence. Farrell, Phillips, and Pease (1995) offer two suggestions as to why it is that particular targets are more likely to be repeatedly involved in crime. The first explanation for repeat victimization is what they refer to as "risk heterogeneity." Victims (or targets) may have certain characteristics that increase the possibility that they will be victimized once and then victimized repeatedly thereafter. These characteristics are thought to exist prior to the initial victimization and are enduring, lasting both before and after initial and later victimizations, regardless of steps that they might take to try to reduce their risk profile. This has been recast in the near repeat literature as "flag victimization."

A second explanation focuses less on the individual characteristics and more on the context in which the victimization takes place. Farrell et al. refer to this as "state dependence" (1995, p. 386). Farrell and his colleagues note: "in the context of re-victimization presumed to be state-dependent, the basic question concerns reasons for the choice of the same [or different] perpetrators offending more than once against the same target[s] in preference to other targets" (p. 386). Rather than enduring traits characterizing victims as in the previous explanation, state dependence implies that victimization changes victims to make them increasingly attractive to offenders. Also, offenders become familiar with the victim and the victim's circumstances, which has been referred to as "boost" victimization in near repeat literature.

In this way, we get increased exposure as the situational context increases the potential for crime. This can be viewed in terms as simple as suggesting that individuals with certain risky experiences find that there is not much they can do to adjust their environment to reduce their risk of victimization. Exposure, then, may come more from frequenting areas where offenders mix with potential victims, preying on one another. Gang- or drug-related shootings are an example of this, whereby the offender one day could be a potential victim the next. But this is obviously not the complete answer. Importantly, the locations in which crimes concentrate are areas that are less desirable to inhabit, especially for people uninterested in behaving illegally. That means that individuals who cannot afford to vacate these locations assume a risk in living there, increasing their chance of victimization and likelihood of revictimization. Urban school-aged children could be one example of such individuals. Victimization occurs in areas such as drug markets that are known as locations of not only high criminal activity, but also high victimization. The violence that emerges in these areas is part of the drug market conditions, but it is also the case that one's very presence in these locations increases exposure to associated crimes, such as robbery, assault, theft, and burglary. This intermixing of crime types in these areas supports the continued incidence of crimes and appearance of hot spots.

HOT SPOTS, NEAR REPEATS, AND SPATIAL VULNERABILITY IN CONTEXT

In studies that have been done to date, researchers have found evidence to support the near repeat phenomenon for a variety of crime types and settings. Investigations of near repeats provide an important extension of hot spot analysis, as they account for the temporal link between crime events and do not just assume that behavior that takes place in close proximity at whatever time in a set frame (for example, a month, a year) has anything to do with other behavior located nearby. As a companion to hot spot analysis, near repeat analysis explains how past crime incidents serve as predictors of new crime incidence. Spelman (1992) concluded that the statistical concentration of crime at places is due to random and often temporary fluctuations in crime events. Nonetheless, even after correcting for such fluctuations, he noted that the worst locations accounted for a disproportionately high number of crime incidents.

Humans are well known to perform actions that can be described as stochastic—that is, irrational, random, or "dumb." Have you ever driven a car on the highway in heavy traffic and, frustrated by the delay, taken an unfamiliar exit in an attempt to circumvent the problematic stretch of roadway? When this misfortune results in a true shortcut, you may do it more often. But other drivers who saw you exit the highway may also have followed you, hoping that you knew a worthwhile detour. Your new travel route may have been a fluke, but now it is your, and maybe others', preferred "new normal" route. Fluctuations in criminal behavior may be the seeds from which new hot spots nucleate and grow. But if places are not ideally suited for crime, then they may never fully mature to be labeled "problem areas" or hot spots. Through independent actions, offenders ultimately converge at the same places over prolonged periods of time to commit similar types of crimes. Why is this so and how do offenders know where to go?

Using the current state of criminological research, we can say that crime event dependence is not a linear process but rather, in the interaction that takes place between crime incidents and context, a constantly changing risk dependence that emerges from the actions of all parties and features of a location. Past crime incidents support future crime occurrence. But what mechanism "allows" crimes to cluster by independent decision makers? We refer, in particular, to the role of the interactions that appear in the collective output (that is, hot spots) of individual offenders who decide to participate in seemingly uncoordinated illegal activities at areas selected by other like-minded individuals. One offender is usually not solely responsible for all the crime events that comprise hot spots. Yet the cohort of offenders in a jurisdiction that a lone offender is part of by virtue of his illegal activity finds, "as a whole," an area that is suitable for crime. This hot spot location tends to be resilient over time, even if one or several contributing individuals are physically removed (for example, arrested) from the location. So, how does this "organization without an organizer" (Garnier, Gautrais, & Theraulaz, 2007, p. 4) operate to cope with uncertain situations and to adapt to activities (for example, hot spots policing, targeted interventions) that threaten the perpetuity of hot spots as desirable criminal behavior settings (Felson, 1995; Taylor & Harrell, 1996)? The mechanism through which disconnected offenders cluster at certain places (that is, by proxy of their crime incidents), despite a seeming lack of deliberate coordination of activities, is understudied and has been ignored in the criminological research literature. We have given this a lot of thought, however, and use an interdisciplinary framework to discuss the intersection of the key ideas about spatial vulnerability from chapters 1 and 2 and those about hot spots and the near repeat exposures, as discussed already in chapter 3.

THE VULNERABILITY-EXPOSURE FRAMEWORK FOR UNDERSTANDING CRIME SYSTEMS

Key properties of self-organized patterns within the study of biology are robustness and flexibility (Garnier et al., 2007). Robustness refers to the ability for a system to perform without failure under a wide range of conditions. Flexibility, like resiliency, refers to the ability of a system to readily adapt to new, different, or changing requirements. To relate this to criminology: crime hot spots tend to be robust and resilient over time. Illegal behaviors of individuals add to the robustness of a hot spot, but the seizure of an offender (or two, or three, or more offenders) from a hot spot area rarely diminishes the overall stability of the hot spot in the long term (Caplan, Kennedy, & Baughman, 2012; Braga, 2005). It may seem as though a hot spot takes on a life of its own, beyond the individual offenders that aided its emergence and, ultimately, helped to sustain its existence, like an invisible deleterious cloud that hovers over part of a city. Ad hoc, short-term, or incomplete police initiatives focused at hot spot areas provide opportunities for illegal actors there to develop a wide range of new collective behaviors, and can be a powerful lever for shaping and optimizing these behaviors in a highly adaptive way. This is especially likely, as Short et al. realized, if the spatial vulnerabilities for crime are homogenous throughout the landscape, which, as we know from the empirical evidence presented in this book, they are not.

A key point here is that interventions by police or other stakeholders at hot spot areas should be robust, sustainable, and flexible (that is, dynamic). Offenders may be aware of global patterns of crime, which inform their decision making and subsequent behaviors. But hot spots nevertheless emerge at the global level from the interactions that take place among individuals at the local level, exhibiting illegal behaviors often for personal rather than communal gain. Repeat offenses at repeat places label criminogenically attractive areas as "problematic" and garner police attention. But interventions focused solely on seizing or otherwise incapacitating offenders located at hot spots will likely fail to cool hot spots because the larger "whole" of offenders can adjust to perturbations (for example, arrests) and will continue to be attracted to these settings. Targeting crime hot spots requires a concerted effort not only to focus on the individual offenders or their victims present there at any given moment in time, but to mitigate the environmental features and their spatial influences that make these areas suitable locations for crime.

What mechanisms operate behind the clustering of illegal behavior to form hot spots in the first place? To be honest, we don't exactly know. But insights lie in the observable patterns and underlying principles of the collective behaviors of offenders. Like a biologist who studies swarms or colonies in nature, we will consider a crime hot spot as a decentralized system made of autonomous units that are distributed in the environment and that may be described as following probabilistic stimulus-response behaviors (Garnier et al., 2007). In this conceptualization, criminals operate on the basis of personal and local information; they have varying probabilities of offending (as measured with actuarial risk assessments); and their behaviors are expected to conform to stimuli of rewards and (risks of) punishments (Cornish & Clarke, 1986). We could add to this conceptualization of a hot spot system that the rules that govern interactions among offenders are executed on the basis of local information, as well as knowledge of the existing global pattern of crime (that is, the hot spot itself). This global knowledge reinforces offenders' personal perceptions of existing hot spot areas to be suitable illegal behavior settings, relative to other places throughout the landscape. Therefore, recent past events and existing crime hot spots significantly affect locations of future crime events. This effect is mediated through considerations of perceptions of features in the environment (that is, spatial vulnerability).

Even in the face of an existing hot spot area, there often remain other suitable places for an offender to commit his crime. Why, then, the collective decision to locate illegal behavior at specific areas in the first place? First, crimes may not always occur at expected high-risk (that is, vulnerable) places or within existing hot spot areas. But, as time passes, the rational choices and stochasticity of individual offenders' decisions yield a few more crimes at the most vulnerable places. The greater number of crimes at these vulnerable places induces a greater number (and veracity) of perceptions that these places are "most suitable" to commit crime and reap rewards. Additional crime events stimulate more offenders to choose these places to commit their crimes. And so on. Information about the local environment guides individual offender activities, which shape the local configuration—pattern—of crime incidents, which in turn influences other specific actions of motivated offenders. Each time an offender commits a new crime, the shape of the local configuration of crime incidents that triggered this action is changed. The new configuration influences other specific actions, and the process continues to form what is ultimately defined by police as a "hot spot." Offenders decide where to add new crime events to the emerging hot spot using the local arrangement of existing known events (that is, contagion). In this way, hot spots emerge from an almost perfect coordination of the collective work of individual offenders who are most likely acting without a well-defined plan but are following relatively simple decision rules that are informed by recent past exposures and spatial vulnerabilities.

The computational simulations of crime occurrence in Los Angeles, California, conducted by Short et al. (2010) demonstrate how some of this might play out, as discussed already. But they failed to account for the heterogeneity of spatial vulnerability and, therefore, for the fact that the potential place ("building site") for a hot spot on a landscape does not have the same probability to be chosen at the outset or reemergence in response to (simulated) intervention activities. There is a greater probability to locate a crime at a highly vulnerable place, and then again near where other crimes already occurred. The building activities resulting in the emergence of a hot spot are driven by individual preferences, available opportunities, and spatial influences of existing environmental features that are detected by the offenders (Grassé, 1959). Once this process begins, the probabilities to start a new hot spot elsewhere—even at another high-risk area—are low. The architecture of a hot spot by itself provides enough information to ensure the coordination of offenders and the persistence of the hot spot.

We have tested this conceptualization of hot spot systems, in collaboration with Simon Garnier, through agent-based modeling. After many simulations, first with training data and then with test data, we found that collective decisions in offenders can arise through the competition between three different types of information that can be amplified in various ways to explain the diversity of hot spots in a jurisdiction. The first type of information regards contagion, which was operationalized as an individual agent's short-term memory that is created by the successful commission of a crime by the agent. The second type of information regards hot spot areas, which were operationalized as collective long-term memory created by every agent's historical knowledge of hot spot areas. The third type of information regards spatial vulnerability, which was operationalized by a relative risk score for places of the landscape (that is, study setting) that were derived from an empirically validated risk terrain model. A successful robbery event, where, for instance, an agent received cash from a victim and was never arrested or punished for it, is a kind of positive feedback that creates the conditions for similar repeat crimes at the same locale and that ultimately clusters at the global level. This parallels the inverse of specific and general deterrence, as discussed in criminological literature. In this case, positive feedback creates specific reinforcement of the illegal behavior among the individual offender (who may repeat his criminal activity at this place) and general reinforcement of the behavior for other current or prospective members of the "hot spot cohort."

We also learned through simulation models that negative feedback counterbalances positive feedback and leads to the stabilization of the collective crime pattern. Negative feedback may have several origins, such as focused police interventions at hot spot places, the swift arrest of a perpetrator, or the mitigation of a criminogenic feature or its spatial influence. Any constraint that modulates the spatial vulnerability or the rate of crime events at an area can lead that area to lose or win its competition against another suitably vulnerable area.

Formal or informal regulation of criminal activity at hot spots reinforces offenders' perceptions of the potential for punishment in probabilistic terms (for example, the more police present, the greater the risk of apprehension). Assuming no discriminatory practices, it also equalizes the playing field, so to speak, for all members of the hot spot cohort. Guided by positive and negative feedback, the hot spot offender cohort adapts its collective behavior through the modulation of individual behaviors. With the term "modulation" we suggest that the probability for a given behavior to occur varies according to the disturbance (for example, temporary vs. sustained police intervention). Each individual is able to sense the variation thanks to local cues and then slightly modifies his or her illegal behavior or site selection in response. These behavioral modifications affect the interaction network, and hence the global structure of the hot spot, through a new balancing of positive and negative feedbacks. When Short et al. simulated a similar scenario on a homogenous risk landscape (that is, where every place is equally suitable for crime), they found that hot spots displace to the immediate surrounding area of the original hot spot quite easily. Through our agent-based simulations on a heterogeneous risk terrain, we realized that crimes are much more likely to emerge away from the intervention activities and within high-risk places. After a short time, crimes began to cluster at these alternate places.

So, hot spots are dynamic systems in that their emergence requires permanent interactions between individual offenders and their environment. These interactions promote the positive feedbacks that create the collective hot spots of crime and act for their subsistence against negative feedbacks that try to eliminate them. Hot spots also display properties that are more complex than the simple contribution of each individual offender. But, in fact, crime hot spots can result from the execution of relatively simple decision rules that guide nonlinear combinations of interactions among individuals. Together with their emergent properties, these nonlinear interactions can also lead hot spots to fragment or even dissolve away altogether when some parameters of the area change. This corresponds to a qualitative change in the collective behavior. But absent a permanent change in a hot spot's parameters, such as mitigating the spatial influences of criminogenic features in a sustained way, it will always attract more offenders. The addition of a social component (Gerber, 2014; Corso, Leroy, & Alsusdais, 2015) of offender interactions (for example, social networking technologies, gang formation, and so on) will likely accelerate the grouping of the individuals around the hot spot and will make the area even more resilient to perturbations (that is, less likely to react to low-intensity police interventions and faster to recover from more intense interventions).

The implications of conceptualizing hot spots as systems suggest that the complexity of crime hot spots in a jurisdiction, which is derived through individual offender activities, does not necessarily require sophisticated individual behavior rules to emerge, persist, or desist. The process is probabilistic, which means that the mechanisms enabling the process can be identified and (presumably) controlled. Successful crime incidents are positive feedback for motivated offenders that amplify "instigator" crime events (Bowers & Johnson, 2005; Johnson et al., 2007; Moreto, Piza, & Caplan, 2014), whether they are the result of intentional or random illegal behavior. Fluctuation of crime incident locations will occur throughout a landscape. But there is a higher probability that crimes will occur and recur at the highest-risk places of the environmental backcloth, as articulated by a risk terrain map.

This vulnerability-exposure framework for studying the spatial dynamics of crime emergence and persistence provides a more holistic view of crime that can be put into action in interventions and prevention strategies. This approach mobilizes analytics that are comprehensive and useful for practical responses to crime problems. It also provides a solid framework for studying risky places. The next chapter sets out the conceptual terms under which we can consider these combined approaches within the context of the Theory of Risky Places.

5

THE THEORY OF RISKY PLACES

RISKY PLACES

Risky places are a product of vulnerability and exposure. They are defined as a function of the combined effect of (1) vulnerability, the spatial influences of features in the environment that contribute to attracting criminal behavior; (2) local exposure, near repeat crime events that occur within a short period of time; and (3) global exposure, areas with a high concentration of criminal incidents. The Theory of Risky Places proposes that risk levels of crime can be computed at places according to the symbiotic effects of these three sets of factors. Spatial vulnerability can be articulated with RTM. Global exposure can be articulated through hot spot mapping. Local exposure can be assessed with near repeat analysis. The Theory of Risky Places considers the interactivity of all three of these evidence-based techniques for modeling the spatial dynamics of crime. It takes the insights of environmental criminology, which looks for the patterns, rhythms, and tempos of criminal behavior, and sets these into a vulnerability-exposure framework that computes the relationship between context, process, and threat. This provides standardized tests for the identification of risky places for crime and a means to test the theory with real data.

McGloin, Sullivan, and Kennedy (2011) suggest that we can increase explanatory power in predicting outcomes by adopting a strategy that considers the interactional effects of crime correlates in encouraging crime emergence. They suggest:

> By adopting analytical tools that explicitly integrate or allow for independent relationships among the elements that produce the outcome, such as simulation models or qualitative

approaches, our ability to understand crime more fully should improve. . . . By using "real data" as a benchmark and grounding for the process—that which we are trying to predict—various decision rules about the ways individual and situational risk interact can be articulated to determine which model generates crime emergence in a real time and space. (p. 11)

Forecasting risky, or likely, locations for crime must incorporate spatial vulnerabilities *and* exposures at micro places if it is to yield the most efficient and actionable information—spatial intelligence. The concept of risk is not new or unique to the criminal justice community, and risk assessment has a long history of being used to identify, prevent, or control crime. High or low risk is often attributed to conventional offender-based risk assessments, first established many decades ago when researchers began to demonstrate that certain characteristics of offenders were correlated with their subsequent behavior. Offender characteristics are scored and combined to form a scale that is indicative of "risk"—such as the risk of rearrest or reconviction, the risk of absconding while on bail, or the risk of violating conditions of parole or probation. Turning attention away from the offender and to the place where crime occurs, the Theory of Risky Places defines risk as a consideration of the probabilities of particular outcomes. A risky place, then, is a particular portion of space that has been assessed for its likelihood of experiencing a particular outcome and to which a value has been attributed, allowing for relative comparisons between places throughout a landscape. As we have argued throughout the book, the concept of risk ties different parts of the crime problem together and offers a probabilistic interpretation to crime analysis.

As an attribute of places, risk for crime is not an absolute value, a dichotomous variable, or a static quotient. It is rarely or never zero. Risk varies in degrees and changes over space and time as public perceptions about environments evolve, as new crimes occur, as police intervene, or as motivated offenders and suitable targets travel. Assessing spatial risks for crime requires a conceptual framework that is attuned to incorporating multiple dynamic factors and producing intelligence that serves strategic decision making and tactical action. The Theory of Risky Places provides such a framework and extends the strong tradition of location-based analysis advocated by researchers, such as Shaw and McKay. It takes advantage of contemporary analytical and technical tools to improve and extend their work. In particular, creating a broader array of responses for police agencies to address crime problems is a primary imperative that runs through all of this work. What the Theory of Risky Places demonstrates is that we can tell police where to go to confront crime but also, using our understanding of exposures and the spatial influences of features in the environment, what to do when they get there.

RESEARCH PROPOSITIONS FOR THE THEORY OF RISKY PLACES

The Theory of Risky Places supports three propositions that are informed by the concepts of spatial influence, spatial inference, and spatial intelligence:

1. All places are at risk, but because of the spatial influence of criminogenic features, some places are riskier than others.

This proposition addresses the direct *spatial influence* that risk factors have on behavior. It is based on Tobler's (1970) first law, but advances what has been done previously, as we look at the relative importance of these factors when considered together rather than as single effects. We can add to this a consideration of risk to suggest that certain types of facilities, known to be stronger attractors of crime, will be where we will find the most crime. A feature's spatial influence can be mapped in a GIS as what we will refer to as a risk map layer.

2. Crime emerges at places when there is high vulnerability based on the combined spatial influences of multiple criminogenic features at said places.

Vulnerability comes from the presence of a combination of spatial influences of features of a landscape that enhance the likelihood of crime. This addresses the concept of *spatial inference,* which regards interactions that occur between features to support criminal behavior. Vulnerability can be operationalized in a GIS as a risk terrain map.

3. Risky places result from an overall assessment of vulnerability and exposures throughout the landscape.

We can say that a place is vulnerable but this is not important if there is no recent nearby exposure to crime. But if crime occurred at a vulnerable place before, then the likelihood that new crimes will occur goes up. These propositions actualize the vulnerability-exposure analytical framework that considers the integration of hot spots, near repeats, and environmental risks, as discussed in chapter 4. We characterize the product of proposition (3) as *spatial intelligence.*

These propositions provide a basis for analyzing the system processes whereby crime emerges, persists, or disappears. For the purposes of testing these propositions, we demonstrate how the Theory of Risky Places informs assessments and actions regarding a crime problem in a way that is consistent with the literature reviewed in previous chapters. We present a test of these propositions using a study of aggravated assault in Chicago. But first, let's explore the joint utility of the analytical techniques of risk terrain modeling, hot spot mapping, and near repeat analysis, which serve as the foundation of the vulnerability-exposure framework.

EXPLORING THE VULNERABILITY-EXPOSURE FRAMEWORK

CASE STUDY 1

Exposure Determined by Hot Spot Mapping

An early test of the vulnerability-exposure framework for crime analysis was completed with our colleague Eric Piza.[1] This research emerged out of collaboration with the New

Jersey State Police (NJSP), looking at data from the calendar years 2007 and 2008 regarding the Township of Irvington, New Jersey, an urban community of about three square miles and a population of approximately 65,000, according to the 2000 census. Murder rates for 2007 were 38.7 per 100,000 persons, compared to a national average of 5.6 (FBI, 2007). The town had a lot of gang-related violence and contained a vibrant drug market. To respond to this violence, the NJSP formed a special task force to supplement the smaller municipal police.

The focus of our study was violent crime, which includes aggravated assault, homicide, robbery, gun shooting, and weapon possession. These were the NJSP task force's targeted crime types in Irvington. Crime data were provided by the NJSP through the Regional Operations Intelligence Center (that is, New Jersey's Fusion Center). There were 57 violent crime incidents from April to August 2007 and 32 violent crime incidents from April to August 2008.[2]

Figure 3 shows where violent crime occurred in the 2007 study period and it demonstrates how crime incidents are not uniformly distributed throughout Irvington.[3] To judge the extent of the apparent clustering, we conducted a Nearest Neighbor (NN) analysis for spatial randomness. The NN analysis calculates the distance from each point in a collection to its nearest neighboring point.[4] These distances are then compared to the expected mean NN distance for a random distribution of points to determine if points are statistically closer than expected under spatial randomness. Violent crimes were significantly clustered in Irvington (Observed Mean = 492.27; Expected Mean = 601.95; NN Ratio = 0.82; Z Score = -2.51; p = 0.01). Given this clustering, we created a kernel density map to identify existing problematic areas and to suggest the areas where violent crimes may likely occur in the future as a function of exposure. A conventional hot spot map is a density map calculated from the locations of crimes from a recent past time period that would then be used to identify existing problematic areas or to suggest the areas where crimes will occur in the future (Harries, 1999). Figure 3 also presents the density map of violent crimes in Irvington from April through August 2007.

The density map is symbolized according to standard deviational breaks, with all places colored in black having density values greater than 2 standard deviations above the mean density value—which statistically puts these places in the top 5% of those most densely populated with violent crimes. As table 4 shows, density hot spot mapping yields respectable place-based forecasts of 2008 violent crimes. In the 100ft × 100ft places on the map in figure 3 that had a density value above 2 standard deviations from the mean in 2007, 17% of violent crime incidents between April and August 2008 occurred within these same places,[5] which total 7% of the area of Irvington.

Exposure Determined by Near Repeat Analysis

Conventional hot spot mapping is atemporal, yet the study of criminogenic places should incorporate time. Near repeat analysis adds a temporal aspect to hot spot analysis by suggesting, with a certain level of statistical confidence, that new crimes happen

April–August 2007 Violent Crimes

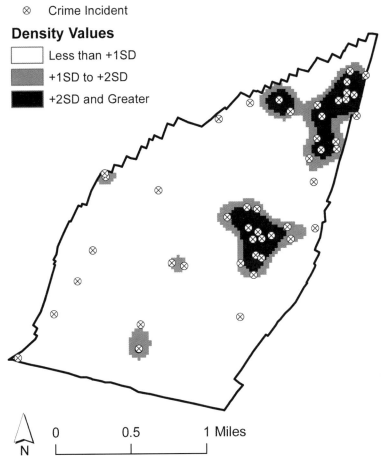

⊗   Crime Incident

Density Values

☐ Less than +1SD

▨ +1SD to +2SD

■ +2SD and Greater

0   0.5   1 Miles

N

FIGURE 3
Violent crime incidents are not evenly distributed throughout Irvington, New Jersey, as shown by the density and point feature layers on this map.

within a certain distance of past crimes and within a certain period of time from the prior incident. According to results of a near repeat analysis of Irvington's violent crime incidents from April through August 2007 using the Near Repeat Calculator,[6] Version 1.3 (Ratcliffe, 2009), we found an overrepresentation of violent crimes at the same place up to seven days after an initial incident ($p < 0.05$). The chance of another violent crime incident was about 500% greater than if there were no repeat victimization pattern.[7] Near repeat violent crimes were also overrepresented between eight and 14 days and within 801 to 900 feet of the initial incident ($p < 0.01$),[8] and there was a 153% greater chance of a new violent crime incident occurring within zero to 14 days at 801 to

TABLE 4   Chi-Squared Results

Place Type (N=4039)	P-Value	Any Violent Crime in 2008 (Yes) (N=30)	Coverage Area of Irvington	Crimes Per Area
Density > +1SD	Fisher's<0.01 Pearson<0.001	12 (41.4%)	1162/8240 cells (14%)	12/1161=0.0103
Density > +2SD	Fisher's=0.098 Pearson=0.095	5 (17.2%)	581/8240 cells (7%)	.0086
Risk Value >= 3	Fisher's<0.001 Pearson<0.001	13 (44.8%)	831/8240 cells (10%)	.0156

NOTE: At least one cell has expected counts less than 5.

900 feet away from the initial incident (p<0.05).[9] History suggests that the spatial-temporal nature of crime incidents in Irvington made certain locations riskier for new crimes to occur than other locations, at certain times.

To further delve into the sequential nature of crime incidents, we need to focus on their time order. In other words, it is important that we can identify a precursor crime that connects to subsequent incidents. Predicting the most likely locations of these "instigator" events requires an understanding of the environment that is most conducive for violent crimes to occur within (Johnson et al., 2007). This brings us to consider spatial vulnerability and argue that characteristics of the environment affect individual-level decisions and criminal behaviors (and vice versa), and ultimately the locations of instigator events. It is therefore appropriate to next consider RTM.

Vulnerability Determined by RTM

Figure 4 presents a risk terrain map for violent crimes that was produced manually, using the ad hoc method, in accordance with the steps described in chapter 2. The map was produced using five risk factor datasets that previous empirical research found to be correlated with violent crime. These risk factors are gang members (Braga, 2004), bus stops (Loukaitou-Sideris, 1999; Roman, 2005; Golledge & Stimson, 1997), schools (Roncek & Maier, 1991; Roncek, 2000), public housing (Newman, 1972; Eck, 1994; Roncek, Bell, & Francik, 1981; Wells, Wu, & Ye, 2011), and facilities of bars, clubs, fast food restaurants, and liquor stores (Brantingham & Brantingham, 1995; Block & Block, 1995; Kennedy, Caplan, & Piza, 2011; Roncek & Maier, 1991; Wells et al., 2011).[10] The risk terrain map is symbolized according to unique risk values, which range from 0 (lowest, green) to 5 (highest, red).

Higher risk places in 2007, according to this risk terrain map, should host violent crime incidents in 2008, unless one or more risky features are mitigated at these places. We were aware that distributions among geographical units, such as raster cells, might

April–August 2007 Risk Terrain

⊗   Violent Crime Incident, Apr – Aug 2008

⊠   Near Repeat Incident, Apr – Aug 2007

Risk Value

▮ 0
▮ 1
▮ 2
▮ 3
▮ 4
▮ 5

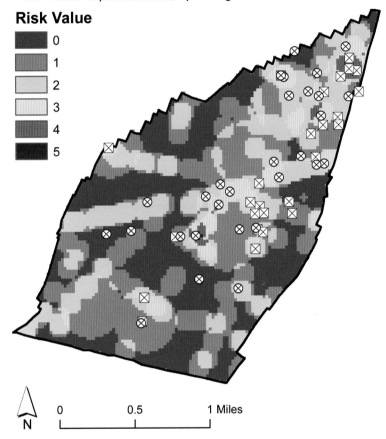

0   0.5   1 Miles

N

FIGURE 4

A risk terrain map for Irvington, New Jersey, showing environmental context for crimes in 2007, layered with near repeat incidents from 2007 and violent crimes from 2008.

not be spatially independent (Anselin, Cohen, Cook, Gorr, & Tita, 2000). A Moran's I test indicated no spatial autocorrelation present, so a spatial lag variable was not created as a control.[11] Our findings suggest that for every unit increase of a place's (that is, cell's) risk value, the likelihood of a violent crime occurring there from April through August 2008 increased by 92%. For places with one or more risk factors in 2007, we can be 95% confident that if violent crimes happen in 2008 the likelihood of them happening at these places is between 37% and 169% greater than other places in Irvington.

We ran a logistic regression where environmental risk was treated as a categorical variable and dummy coded; zero (0) risk was the reference category. Risk values equal to or greater than three were significant predictors of future shootings compared to values of zero.[12] The order of magnitude for risk values' effect sizes confirms that the more spatial vulnerability present at a place, the greater the likelihood of a future violent crime occurring there. In reference to table 4, nearly 45% of all violent crimes in 2008 happened at places with risk values of three or more, which comprised 10% of the area of Irvington.[13]

In looking at these results, it appeared to us that occurrences of violent crimes in 2008 at places where violent crimes produced hot spots in 2007 were attributable to criminogenic stagnation. That is, risk factors at places stayed the same or were not successfully mitigated over time. The locations of schools, bars, and the like did not change drastically from year to year. If spatial influences of risk factors in the risk terrain model are not directly and successfully mitigated, and crimes continue to occur, then they will likely cluster at the same vulnerable places over time, creating hot spots. In this way, as presented above, crime hot spots were valid measures of where new crimes were likely to occur in the future because they were proxy measures of environments that were chronically most conducive to illegal violent behavior.

Testing the Joint Utility of Hot Spot Mapping, Near Repeat Analysis, and RTM

Results from the previous sections suggest that police in Irvington could have strategically allocated resources to key crime-infested places, given their knowledge of where violent crimes were concentrating at hot spots and the time frame and general area within which near repeat crimes were likely to occur. RTM could be used to identify criminogenic features of the landscape that correlate with these violent crime incidents, and then used to empirically test the effect of their combined spatial influences on criminal behavior. The joint utility of these crime analysis techniques offers police a unique opportunity to suppress violent crimes immediately by allocating resources to existing hot spots. They can, in addition, aim to prevent violent crimes through interventions at high-risk places, even if violent crimes are not yet occurring there.

To test the joint utility of hot spot mapping and RTM, an analysis was conducted to measure the effect of the "presence of any violent crimes from April through August 2007" on the locations of violent crimes from April through August 2008 (see figure 4). At the microlevel unit of analysis, 2007 violent crime incidents were a significant predictor of 2008 violent crime incident locations.[14] This finding is consistent with the conceptual framework of hot spot mapping, the conclusions of empirical research regarding hot spots (for example, Chainey, Tompson, & Uhlig, 2008; Gorr & Olligschlaeger, 2002), and the decisions by police commanders to allocate resources to high-crime places. But including a measure of environmental risk yields an even better model of future violent crime locations compared to predictions made with past violent crime incidents alone. Places in Irvington with past violent crimes had a 478% increased likelihood of future violent crimes compared to places that were not host to violent crimes in the previous year, when controlling for environmental risk. Places with risk values of 3 or more had a 458% increase in the likelihood of future violent crimes compared to places with lower risk values, when controlling for the presence of prior violent crime incidents. These results were statistically significant and confirm that violent crimes occur at high-risk places, particularly those where violent crimes already occurred.

The joint applications of RTM and near repeat analysis can be used to anticipate the spatial and temporal limits of near repeat events that follow unpreventable violent crime incidents. According to results of the near repeat analysis, near repeat violent crimes were most likely to occur between 801 and 900 feet and within 14 days of an instigator event. Near repeat incidents from April through August 2007 were most likely to happen at higher-risk places within these bounds (see figure 4). Environmental risk (that is, spatial vulnerability) remains significant to the locations of near repeats even when controlling for the presence of instigator events at places. This finding supports the near repeat phenomena and the relationship it has with environmental risks above and beyond crime incidents themselves. "Risk heterogeneity" of environments, as articulated by risk terrain maps, exists prior to the initial victimization and can be enduring without proper intervention efforts. So, "state dependence" exists at places with instigator crimes, which makes the same target or nearby targets especially attractive. Where risk heterogeneity and state dependence coexist, that is, when instigator events locate in risky places, the emergence of new crimes is especially likely.

Considering all the results from this study, we surmised that violent crimes that cannot be prevented and that serve as instigator events (for near repeats) are most likely to attract near repeat incidents at nearby places of high vulnerability, as opposed to places within the expected near repeat bandwidth that have very low risk (as illustrated in figure 5). Stated another way, instigator violent crimes may create a "pie" of a certain radius within which near repeat incidents are most likely to happen during a certain time frame. But within this pie, some "slices" are more likely to have violent crimes than other slices. A separate and subsequent study of burglary crimes in Newark, New Jersey, arrived at a similar conclusion (Moreto, Piza, & Caplan, 2014).

One advantage of knowing that a near repeat phenomenon exists for violent crimes in a jurisdiction and that violent crimes are more likely to occur at high-risk places is the ability to prioritize each new crime incident according to its propensity for being the instigator event for near repeat crimes. Assuming that every new violent crime incident is a potential instigator for near repeats, priority can be given to new crimes that occur at higher-risk places with other high-risk places in close proximity. This joint utility of information derived from hot spot mapping, near repeat analysis, and risk terrain modeling got us thinking about the decision rules that govern behaviors at crime incident locations and initiated our journey toward thinking about the vulnerability-exposure framework and, ultimately, the development of the Theory of Risky Places.

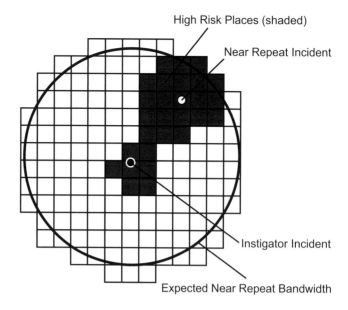

FIGURE 5

Instigator violent crimes create a bandwidth within which near repeat incidents are most likely to happen at environmentally risky places.

TESTING THE PROPOSITIONS OF THE THEORY OF RISKY PLACES
CASE STUDY 2

In research conducted on data from Chicago (Kennedy, Caplan, Piza, & Buccine-Schraeder, 2015) we expanded on the Irvington study reported above in order to specifically test the three propositions of the Theory of Risky Places. We found that by articulating spatial vulnerability and considering it in the context of spatial exposures, the Theory of Risky Places helps guide analyses that identify and prioritize specific areas and features of the landscape that should be addressed by a targeted intervention (Kennedy & Caplan, 2014). The theory not only considers the role that changing situational factors might have on crime outcomes; it also provides a means to evaluate the overall effect of the risks presented by features that have strong influence in creating vulnerability and increased exposure to crime. Using analytical tools that are consistent with the vulnerability-exposure framework, one can apply the theory to identify criminogenic features and their interaction with hot spots and near repeats to create risky places. These places should be the locations that are targeted for change and prevention activities. We will present the findings of this study here to show how the theory holds up to analytical scrutiny. This is offered as an introduction to the ways in which risky places can be operationalized.

Chicago was the focus of study by Shaw and McKay over a number of decades and serves as a compelling setting for our discussion of the Theory of Risky Places. It is one of the major cities in the United States and is the largest city in Illinois, with a long history of serious crime problems. In 2012 Chicago suffered a spike in homicides and gun violence incidents. The dramatic jump to 500 homicides in the city—a 16% increase compared to 2011—prompted city officials to rethink policing strategies. Street crime, in particular aggravated assault, is an ongoing problem in the city. While a single part 1 crime category, aggravated assault covers a wide range of criminal behaviors, from shootings to beatings in which victims sustain serious injuries. In Chicago there were over 12,000 aggravated assaults in 2012, giving us a large number of incidents to examine across the large expanse of the city. Aggravated assaults provide a good test of the Theory of Risky Places, as they have been the focus of other place-based research (Scott & Dedel, 2006). Aggravated assault also offers the chance to test the contextual effects of place on "street" crime.

Risk factors for this study were selected based on the empirical research evidence and the knowledge of personnel at the Chicago Police Department, who provided practical experience-based justification for the use of some factors. This selection followed the advice of Ratcliffe and McCullagh (1998), who argue that the experience of analysts and practitioners should be considered in order to unravel potentially relevant factors. Initially, there were 23 risk factors identified for inclusion in the study: apartment complexes, automatic teller machines (ATMs), foreclosures, gas stations, gas stations with convenience stores,[15] grocery stores, healthcare centers and gymnasiums, homeless shelters, Laundromats, post offices, recreation centers, rental halls, retail shops, variety stores, 3–1-1 service requests about abandoned vehicles, 3–1-1 service requests about street lights being all out, schools, gang hot spots, bars, liquor stores, nightclubs, problem buildings, and bus stops (Scott & Dedel, 2006; Madensen & Eck, 2008; Maguire, 2007; Hunter & Jeffery, 1997; Roncek & Faggiani, 1985; Rengert, Ratcliffe, & Chakravorty, 2005; Stucky & Ottensmann, 2009; Brantingham & Brantingham, 1995; Block & Block, 1995; Clarke & Eck, 2005; Eck, Clark, & Guerette, 2007; Kennedy et al., 2011). Data on business facilities were obtained from InfoGroup (2010). Other data were obtained from the Chicago Police Department (CPD), along with point-level crime data for the calendar years 2011 and 2012. Calls-for-service (3–1-1) data were obtained from the City of Chicago's Data Portal (https://data.cityofchicago.org).

Testing Proposition 1

In testing proposition (1) using the RTMDx Utility, we found that 13 risk factors had significant spatial associations with aggravated assault incidents according to their spatial influences. In order of their RRVs, the factors are problem buildings, known gang territories, foreclosures, bus stops, liquor stores, bars, grocery stores, gas stations, schools, 3–1-1 service requests for street lights being all out, apartment complexes, 3–1-1 service requests about abandoned vehicles, and variety stores. The most meaningful operationalizations and spatial influential distances of each risk factor are presented in table 5. The RRVs can be easily compared. For instance, a place influenced by problem buildings has an expected rate of crime that is twice as high as a place influenced by

TABLE 5   Risk Factors, Spatial Influences, and Relative Risk Values of the Risk
Terrain Model

Risk Factor	Spatial Influence (Operationalization)	Coefficient	Relative Risk Value
Problem Buildings	426ft (Proximity)	1.0458	2.84
Gang Hot Spots	852ft (Proximity)	0.9284	2.53
Foreclosures	852ft (Proximity)	0.9210	2.51
Bus Stops	426ft (Density)	0.5704	1.76
Liquor Stores	426ft (Density)	0.5208	1.68
Bars	426ft (Density)	0.4185	1.51
Grocery Stores	852ft (Density)	0.3535	1.42
Gas Stations	1278ft (Proximity)	0.2547	1.29
Schools	1278ft (Proximity)	0.2376	1.26
3–1-1 Requests for All Street Lights Out	852ft (Proximity)	0.2255	1.25
Apartment Complexes	1278ft (Proximity)	0.1680	1.18
3–1-1 Requests for Abandoned Vehicles	1278ft (Proximity)	0.1676	1.18
Variety Stores	1278ft (Proximity)	0.1504	1.16
Intercept	–	–4.1625	–

grocery stores (RRVs: 2.84 / 1.42 = 2). Accordingly, as posited in proposition (1), all places may have some risk of crime occurrence, but because of the spatial influence of certain criminogenic features, certain places are riskier than others.

Testing Proposition 2

Proposition (2) posits that new crime incidents are likely to emerge at places when there is a high vulnerability based on the combined spatial influences of multiple criminogenic features at said places. We found that when combined in a GIS map, places with risk scores one standard deviation above the mean risk score have 131% increased likelihood of experiencing aggravated assaults. Places with RRSs two standard deviations above the mean (that is, the top 5% of high risk) have 206% increased likelihood of experiencing aggravated assaults.

These results suggest that the risk terrain map produced to articulate the environmental backcloth for aggravated assaults in Chicago was statistically valid. The empirical predictive validity of the risk terrain model supports proposition (2) because places that are most vulnerable on the map are also places where future aggravated assaults occurred most often. Higher-risk places have an exceptionally strong likelihood of experiencing future crime incidents.

Having considered the importance of spatial influence and the concentration of these effects in risk terrain maps, we have a basis upon which to identify vulnerability and forecast crime emergence using this vulnerability. However, crime does not always occur at the most vulnerable places. Exceptions can be due to a number of factors. For example, as we explained in previous chapters, places may be high-risk, but motivated offenders may not be present simultaneous to suitable victims or targets. Or steps may have been taken to reduce crime, hence reducing exposure. If we consider that the expansion of crime prevention activities could lead to the eradication of risky places, we would want to develop a strategy for modeling these and adding them to crime forecasts as a function of vulnerability *and* exposure. Proposition (3) posits that risky places result from an overall assessment of vulnerability and exposures throughout the landscape.

Using the near repeat calculator, we found that repeat victimization and near repeats were present for aggravated assaults in Chicago in 2012. There was a 279% (statistically significant, p < 0.05) greater likelihood of the same location experiencing an aggravated assault within seven days of an initial incident. Additionally, there was a 40% (p < 0.05) greater chance of locations within 426 feet (one block) and within seven days of an instigator incident experiencing aggravated assault incidents. Essentially, near repeat aggravated assaults were most likely to occur within one block and one week of an instigator event.

Given this finding of a near repeat phenomenon, instigator and near repeat incidents were noted accordingly in the attribute table of the point shapefile of all 2012 aggravated assaults in Chicago.[16] Buffers with a radius of 426 feet were drawn around each aggravated assault incident point feature to connote the expected area for near repeat incidents to occur within seven days. Average risk (that is, average vulnerability) for each buffer area was calculated based on the average risk score of cells from the risk terrain map that intersected each buffer, as illustrated in figure 6. The average risk score for all buffer areas was 32.56 (n = 7,883, standard deviation = 19.76). The average risk score for buffer areas of *noninstigator* aggravated assault incidents was 32.04 (n = 7,173, standard deviation = 19.72). The average risk score for buffer areas of *instigator* aggravated assault incidents was 38.82 (n = 600; standard deviation = 19.26).

These differences in means between noninstigator and instigator incidents were significant at p<0.001, according to results from an independent samples t-test. They are also practically meaningful in that aggravated assault incidents that become instigators for near repeats occur at places surrounded by above-average risk. Alternatively, aggravated assault incidents that do not attract near repeats occur at places surrounded by below-average risk. This finding suggests that the overall effect of risky places on crime is a function of vulnerability and exposure throughout the landscape, and lends strong support to proposition (3) of the Theory of Risky Places.

These results conceptualize the relationships between criminogenic features of landscapes that lead to the formation of suitable places for illegal behavior. Risky places are

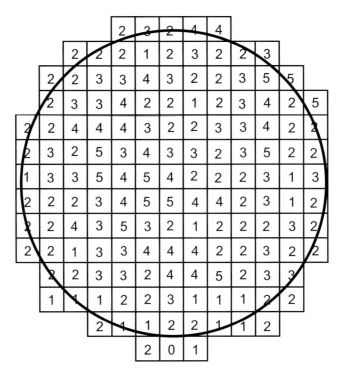

FIGURE 6

As illustrated, average risk for each buffer around crime incidents was
calculated as the mean risk score of cells from the risk terrain map
that intersected each buffer. Shown here: n cells = 148; mean risk
value of buffer area = 2.60.

formed as a result of the confluence of the spatial influences of certain factors combined
with conditions of exposure derived from past crime events. It is clearly not enough to
assume that the risk of crime at places increases because crime occurred there already,
or because there was an absolute increase in crime counts throughout a macro area.
What is more likely is that the risk of crime increases at places with certain spatial qualities that attract motivated offenders and are conducive to certain illegal behaviors.

DISCUSSION

These two case studies demonstrate that the combined effects of vulnerability and exposure lead to the identification of risky places. We have demonstrated the value of this
approach and the extent to which it facilitates targeting places and crime for intervention. In testing the relative efficacy of hot spot analysis and RTM, Drawve (2014) empirically established that while the former is more accurate in targeting locations of future
crime, the latter is more precise in long-term forecasts. He suggests that this occurs due
to the fact that the presence of crime in an area preconditions it to more crime. However,

the stability of these events over time is low. The effects of risk factors measured through RTM are less likely to change over time and, therefore, the precision of predictions of future crimes is enhanced. What reduces the accuracy of RTM is the fact that high-risk areas may not see any crime at all and, therefore, generate false positives. But this is exactly what we have been discussing above. Vulnerability to crime, as measured through RTM, does not always result in actual victimization. Exposure, as measured through event-based approaches like hot spot mapping and near repeat analysis, targets those areas where vulnerability is high. Adopting the two approaches to understand crime patterns and to forecast new crime locations increases both accuracy and precision (see Kennedy et al., 2011; Caplan et al., 2013a). Next, we consider event analysis as a way to interpret the situational aspects of risky places.

6

EVENT CONTEXTS
OF RISKY PLACES

In this chapter we discuss how risky places, which are a product of both vulnerability and exposure, are best understood when interpreted within event contexts. Sacco and Kennedy (2002) proposed looking at crime from an event perspective. This not only considers the incident that occurs but examines crime in the context of the situational factors that precede the incident and its aftermath. This allows the analyst to identify conditions under which certain interactions take place, and then to consider effects that the incident has on victims, offenders, bystanders, and others over time. The criminal event perspective has been used in work on victimization (Wilcox & Gialopsos, 2015), terrorism (Van Brunschot & Kennedy, 2008), violent crime (Kennedy & Forde, 1998), and property crime. The event perspective resonates with the work on situational crime prevention (and extensions thereof; Zahm, 2007; Clarke, 1997), and by Wortley (2008) who uses the concept of "precipitators" as a source that is needed for crime to emerge. Precipitators are "events and influences that occur prior to the contemplated behavior" that can "supply or intensify the motivation for individuals to commit crime" (p. 52). Accordingly, the immediate environment need only enable the performance of illegal behavior; situational precipitators initiate it. Wortley (2008) used the following scenario with the character of Jim to suggest how immediate environments can actively encourage or induce individuals to commit crimes, even if they were not otherwise contemplated:

> Jim arranges to meet his friends at a local nightclub for an evening out. He arrives at the club in good spirits anticipating an enjoyable night. When he arrives at the front door, the

door staff are surly and belligerent towards him before eventually allowing him to go inside. When he enters the nightclub he discovers it is packed to capacity. After fighting his way through the crowd he finally locates his friends. There are no tables or chairs left and they are forced to stand in the corner with people jostling around them. The music is at full volume and continues without a break, making it impossible to carry on a conversation. The air conditioning cannot cope with the crowd and the room is hot, dark and oppressive. Jim and his friends drink steadily. However, getting to the bar is an ordeal and it can take half an hour to get served. As Jim struggles back from the bar with the latest round of drinks, another patron bumps him and knocks the drinks all over him. Jim's friends urge him to retaliate and hit the man. (p. 48)

Since arriving at the nightclub, Wortley explains, Jim had experienced a series of stresses and frustrations that primed him for aggression. The spilled drinks were the final straw. If Jim's drinks were spilled, but Jim was in a good mood prior to then, he may have been more inclined to accept the spill as an accident. As it was, "the probability of a violent response was significantly increased by a variety of situational precipitators" that helped to explain changes in criminal propensity within the individual (Wortley, 2008, p. 49).

As with conventional offender-based risk assessment, whose principles were established many decades ago when research began to demonstrate that characteristics of offenders were correlated with their subsequent behavior (Burgess, 1928; Glueck & Glueck, 1950; Miller & Lin, 2007), precipitators alone do not reliably predict who will and who will not offend. They all have substantial margins of error in this regard. But a situational-based understanding, or event context, of crime incidents combined with the principles of the Theory of Risky Places presents a holistic way of looking at behavioral outcomes as less deterministic and as more a function of a dynamic interaction among people that occurs at places.

As an illustration of this, we examine how an event perspective applies when considering the case of officer safety and the situational factors that enhance or reduce the likelihood of officers being injured on the job. In 2012, homicides and batteries of law enforcement officers occurred predominantly at private residences, nightclubs, and bars in circumstances in which officers were attempting to arrest suspects or investigating calls of suspicious activity (Covington, Huff-Corzine, & Corzine, 2014; FBI, 2012; International Association of Chiefs of Police [IACP], 2011). In the case of calls-for-service, pedestrian stops, traffic stops, or other police interactions with the general public, a precipitator may be the police officer's arrival on scene, attempt to make an arrest, or any other interference with a persons' intended activities (Wortley, 2001, 2002; Caplan, 2003). Physiological reactions to such interferences may lead to aggressive behavior against police officers (Wortley, 2008; Berkowitz, 1983). Since calls-for-service can originate at nearly any place within a jurisdiction, the vulnerability-exposure framework can be combined with the event perspective for analytical efforts aimed at mitigating occupational hazards of policing.

Police officers in the United States have nearly 63 million annual contacts with the general public (Langton & Durose, 2011). In every one of these events, the assessment and management of risk are an operational imperative. While the goal of many police agencies over the decades has been to be the ever-present "capable guardians," a police officer's presence can become a new target of aggression and violence, making the officer the potential victim (Wortley, 2008). Police must appraise the risk of physical injury in every call-for-service or other contact with the people they serve. To that specific end, police actions must be tactical, carefully tailored for use in immediate support of policing operations in accordance with the known facts and conditions relevant to an event. In this or other similar scenarios beyond policing—where thoughtful responses and purposeful actions with an immediate end in view are required—the holistic assessment of risk is critical.

Building on what is known about spatial risk factors for felonious injury to law enforcement officers in the United States, we begin this case study, completed in collaboration with Phillip Marotta and Eric Piza, by producing a risk terrain model for battery and assault to municipal police officers in Chicago, Illinois.[1] We show how battery/assault to police officers could occur time and again without any evidence of significant spatial clustering. So, the question to be answered with RTM is: "Do battery/assault incidents share common spatial correlates of the landscape upon which they occur?" Here, we demonstrate how RTM produces evidence-based spatial intel that law enforcement can use to assess and manage their own risks of personal injury at places throughout their jurisdictions. We advance this discussion by considering spatial vulnerabilities and exposures with event context to develop a comprehensive understanding of risk that can inform strategic and tactical decision making for thoughtful action.

On January 31, 1835, the State of Illinois authorized the Town of Chicago to establish its own police force. Today, the Chicago Police Department (CPD) is the second largest local law enforcement agency in the United States (behind New York City) with 4.4 sworn officers per 1,000 residents, or about 12,000 sworn officers (Chicago Police Department, 2010). The city is divided into 25 police districts. Each district has between nine and 15 police beats, with a total of 277 beats throughout the City. It is at the beat level that the department's strategies for problem solving are implemented (Chicago Police Department, 2010).

This case study focuses primarily on incidents of battery to police officers in Chicago during 2012.[2] These include battery with a weapon (nonfirearm) (N = 110) and battery with serious injury (N = 26). Considering the exceptionally serious nature of threatening a police officer with a firearm, even if the trigger is not pulled or an officer is not struck with a bullet, both batteries and assaults with a firearm (N = 76) were used to assess locations where guns, in general, tend to be used aggressively against police and where there is great potential for extreme physical harm. All battery/assault incidents were also studied (N = 991) as a comprehensive category. For consistency,[3] we

TABLE 6   Spatial Patterns of Battery/Assault Categories

Outcome Event (CY 2012)	Observed Mean	Expected Mean	NN Ratio	Z Score	Spatial Pattern
All Battery/Assault	884.44	1566.90	.56	−26.23**	Clustered
Battery/Assault with Firearm	4039.74	4358.60	.92	−1.22	Random
Battery with a Weapon	3410.90	3911.32	.87	−2.56*	Clustered
Battery, Serious Injury	9623.01	6782.08	1.41	4.08**	Dispersed

*p<0.05

**p<0.001

henceforth use the term "battery/assault" to connote an act in which an assailant intentionally causes serious bodily harm or death to law enforcement in the line of duty.

EXPOSURE: SPATIAL CLUSTERING OF BATTERY/ASSAULT INCIDENTS

Visual inspection of the incident locations of battery/assault to police officers in Chicago suggests that these events are not uniformly distributed and may be clustered in certain areas. As shown in table 6, results of a Nearest Neighbor (NN) analysis suggest that the distribution of all incidents of battery/assault to police officers (N = 991) and battery to police officers with a weapon (nonfirearm) (N = 110), respectively, are significantly spatially clustered. However, battery/assault to police officers with a firearm (N = 76) and battery resulting in serious injury to police officers (N = 26) are not clustered.

Battery/assault to police officers is one particular crime that departments seek to minimize and control before it becomes endemic. Police officers patrol and respond to calls-for-service in all parts of Chicago. So, to some degree, all police officers throughout the entire jurisdiction are exposed to the possibility of battery/assault in the line of duty. It is clear from the NN analysis that battery/assault against police officers could become problematic without any evidence of the significant spatial clustering of incidents. For types of battery/assault incidents that do not cluster, knowledge of spatial risks can be especially meaningful in that police officers could assess risk of battery/assault given certain characteristics of the environment even if such incidents have not yet occurred. The question to be answered next is whether the four categories of battery/assault against police officers share common spatial correlates of the landscape upon which they occur.

POTENTIAL SPATIAL RISK FACTORS

A review of empirical studies, publicly available agency safety protocols, in-service training materials, policy reports, research publications, and briefs points to several spatial factors that may generally elevate the likelihood that an officer will sustain injury in the process of managing a variety of types of calls-for-service. Locations with high rates of prior violent crimes or concentrations of gang members, drug distributors, or illegal drug markets afford suspects with opportunity to elicit assistance from others in evasion or attack, thereby elevating the risk of physical battery or fatality to police (California Commission on Police Officer Standards and Training [POST], 2001; IACP, 2003; Kaminski, Jefferis, & Gu, 2003; Kaminski, 2007; Meyer & Carroll, 2013).

Terrain that is not level, tall brush, residential yards, walls, fences, sharp turns, and open areas where it is hard to construct a perimeter all constitute potential spatial risk factors for injury, especially during foot pursuit (Detroit Police Department, 2010; IACP, 2003). Areas with remote or secluded geographic locations and confined spaces are also locations with high risks for battery/assault (POST, 2001; IACP, 2003). In cases of ambush, fleeing suspects capitalize on available abandoned vehicles as hiding places. Roadways with limited lighting have been shown to restrict an officer's ability to assess risk and provide spatial opportunities for suspects to initiate violent behavior (National Highway Traffic Safety Administration [NHTSA], 2011). Large, unlocked buildings or abandoned lots (IACP, 2003; Shane, 2012) or mobile homes or residential structures that are detached or secluded can enable suspects to evade police attention and facilitate successful ambush (Detroit Police Department, 2010; IACP, 2003; R. Johnson, 2008). Small apartment complexes require law enforcement officers to enter enclosed spaces, providing inadequate distance between the officer and the suspect to ensure safety (Kaminski & Sorensen, 1995).

Areas with high concentrations of locations of psychiatric and social service provisions also present potential risk factors for officer injury. This is not because of an inherent potential for violence attributed to the mental health condition itself, but rather because of the spatial-temporal context presented by high concentrations of service provision agencies in charge of distributing a limited supply of essential resources (Cordner, 2006). Cordner (2006) suggests that the agitation imposed by waiting long hours for medications and "drawing straws" to receive essential services, such as shelter services, increases the likelihood of violence. Clinics, group homes, and shelters are all examples of locations with elevated risk of combative, resistant, or violent behaviors toward law enforcement officers in these regards (Cordner, 2006).

Due to the volatile nature of liquor consumption and crowd density, nightclubs and bars are locations where combative and assaultive behaviors often cluster (Scott & Dedel, 2006; Block & Block, 1995; Covington et al., 2014; FBI, 2012; IACP, 2011). Studies suggest that violence clusters in close proximity to drinking establishments—in streets, on sidewalks, in alleys, and in parking lots—but it is the liquor establishment that is the spatial anchor radiating risk into the immediate surroundings. Banks, poorly lit parking lots, and pharmacies are other locations where law enforcement officers have been killed or assaulted in the line of duty (POST, 2001; IACP, 2011).

Although a broad spectrum of environmental features may pose general spatial risks to police officers in the line of duty, it is likely that only some of them will be significantly influential to battery/assault against police officers within Chicago. A risk terrain model can assess this.

RTM methods were detailed in chapter 2, so the steps will not be itemized here. Potential features of the Chicago landscape that may correlate with battery/assault during the calendar year 2012 were selected based on the empirical research evidence presented in the section above, and the knowledge of personnel at the Chicago Police Department who provided practical experience-based justification for the use of some factors. Initially, 25 measures were identified and accessible as possible risk factors. Regarding "limited visibility," 3–1-1 service requests for street lights out and 3–1-1 service requests for alley lights out were obtained from Chicago's Data Portal. Regarding "areas where criminal actors congregate," gang hot spots were obtained from the Chicago Police Department. Regarding "landscape hazards," 3–1-1 service requests for abandoned vehicles, schools, and parks were obtained from Chicago's Data Portal; the latter two often have fields and open spaces that may be difficult to construct a perimeter around. Related to the "built environment," data on apartment complexes, foreclosed houses, problem buildings,[4] nightclubs, bars, liquor stores, homeless shelters, mental health care providers, substance abuse treatment facilities, recovery homes, recreation centers, pharmacies, parking garages, retail shops, variety stores, and banks were obtained from the Chicago Police Department, Chicago's Data Portal, or Infogroup. Measures such as Laundromats, grocery stores, or gas stations with convenience stores are included due to their often high crowd density, long hours of operation, or scarcity of agents of control. In consultation with the Chicago Police Department, these data were considered appropriate and representative measures of the "general pool" of risk factors that were identified in the literature review above.

Chicago was modeled as a continuous raster grid of 426ft by 426ft cells (N = 36,473), each representing a place throughout the city. This spatial dimension corresponds to the mean block face length of Chicago's street network and is likely the most realistic unit that police can be deployed to at the micro level. Practical micro units of analysis are especially important here since most felonious batteries/assaults occur when the assailant is less than 10 feet away from the police officer.

To identify the optimal spatial influence of each of the 25 risky features, we used the RTMDx Utility to measure whether each raster cell was within 426ft, 852ft, or 1,278ft of the feature point or in an area of high density of the feature points based on a kernel density bandwidth of 426ft, 852ft, or 1,278ft feet. This process generated 117 variables of spatial influence measured as a function of Euclidean distance or kernel density at up to 1, 2, or 3 blocks from each risk factor, which was then tested for spatial correlations with incident locations of battery/assault to police officers in Chicago during the calendar year 2012. Relative risk values were produced for comparison among the significant risk factors in the final risk terrain model.

RTM for All Batteries/Assaults, 2012

The best risk terrain model was a Negative Binomial model with 11 risk factors. In order of their relative risk values, the factors are foreclosures, problem buildings, bars, schools, gang territories, banks, apartment complexes, liquor stores, 3–1-1 service requests for street lights all out, grocery stores, and retail shops. The most meaningful operationalizations and spatial influential distances of each risk factor are presented in table 7. The relative risk values can be easily compared. For instance, a place influenced by problem buildings has an expected rate of crime that is nearly twice as high as a place influenced by 3–1-1 service requests for street lights all out (RRVs: 3.00 / 1.48 = 2.02). Accordingly, all places may pose risk of battery/assault to officers when dealing with a variety of types of calls-for-service at these locations, but because of the spatial influence of certain features of the landscape, some places are riskier than others.

Places where the spatial influence of more than one of these 11 features colocates pose a higher risk: Relative risk scores for each cell in the risk terrain map ranged from one for the lowest risk cell to 582 for the highest risk cell. A cell with a value of 582 has an expected rate of battery/assault that is 582 times higher than a cell with a value of one. The mean risk value is 15.33, with a standard deviation of 23.60.

RTM for Battery/Assault with a Firearm, 2012

Battery/assault with a firearm (that is, handgun or rifle) against police officers occurred 76 times in Chicago during 2012. Four of these incidents were battery. The best risk terrain model for incidents of battery/assault to police officers with a firearm included three risk factors. In order of their relative risk values, the factors are gang territory, problem buildings, and foreclosures (table 7). Places where the spatial influence of more than one of these features colocates pose an even higher risk to police officers: Relative risk scores for each cell in the risk terrain map ranged from one for the lowest-risk cell to 37 for the highest-risk cell. The mean risk value is 6.35, with a standard deviation of 9.96.

RTM for Battery with a Weapon (Nonfirearm), 2012

Battery with a weapon (nonfirearm) occurred 110 times to Chicago police officers in 2012. The best risk terrain model for battery with a weapon to police officers included five risk factors. In order of their relative risk values, the factors are apartment complexes, problem buildings, bars, gang territory, and liquor stores (see table 7). Places where the spatial influence of more than one of these features colocates pose a higher risk to police officers: Relative risk scores for each cell in the risk terrain map ranged from one for the lowest risk cell to 152 for the highest risk cell. The mean risk value is 3.85, with a standard deviation of 7.68.

TABLE 7   Risk Factors, Spatial Influences, and Relative Risk Values of the Risk Terrain Models

Risk Factor	All Battery/Assault SI, Op., Coef., RRV	w/ Firearm SI, Op., Coef., RRV	w/ Other Weapon SI, Op., Coef., RRV	w/ Serious Injury SI, Op., Coef., RRV
Foreclosures	1278, P, 1.95, 7.08	426, P, 1.15, 3.17	–	–
Problem Buildings	852, D, 1.10, 3.00	1278, D, 1.19, 3.29	852, D, 1.37, 3.94	852, D, 2.17, 8.81
Bars	426, D, 0.85, 2.35	–	426, D, 1.20, 3.33	–
Schools	426, D, 0.70, 2.02	–	–	–
Gang Territory	1278, P, 0.63, 1.88	1278, P, 1.26, 3.56	1278, P, 1.10, 3.00	–
Banks	426, P, 0.61, 1.85	–	–	–
Apartment Complexes	426, P, 0.53, 1.70	–	426, D, 1.62, 5.08	–
Liquor Stores	852, D, 0.46, 1.59	–	852, P, 0.92, 2.52	–
3–1-1 Service Requests for Street Lights All Out	426, D, 0.39, 1.48	–	–	–
Grocery Stores	852, D, 0.36, 1.43	–	–	–
Retail Shops	1278, P, 0.28, 1.32	–	–	–
Intercept Coefficient	−6.4031	−8.0262	−7.1814	−7.8951

ABBREVIATIONS: SI=Spatial Influence (in Feet); Op.=Operationalization (P=Proximity; D=Density); Ceof.=Coefficient; RRV=Relative Risk Value

NOTE: Other factors tested, but not included in any model: 3–1-1 Service Requests for Abandoned Vehicles, 3–1-1 Service Requests for Alley Lights Out, Gas Stations with Convenience Stores, Homeless Shelters, Laundromats, Nightclubs, Parking Stations/Garages, Parks, Pharmacies, Recreation Centers, Variety Stores, Mental Health Care Providers, Recovery Homes, Substance Abuse Treatment Facilities.

RTM for Battery with Serious Injury, 2012

Battery resulting in serious injury to police officers occurred 26 times in Chicago during 2012. This represents 2.6% of the total incidents of battery to police officers in 2012. The best risk terrain model for incidents of serious injury to police officers from battery has one risk factor. The factor is problem buildings (see table 7). Places where the spatial influence of problem buildings exists poses a higher risk of serious injury to police officers: Relative risk scores for each cell in the risk terrain map ranged from one for the lowest risk cell to nearly 9 for the highest risk cell. The mean risk value is 1.91, with a standard deviation of 2.51.

CONSIDERING BOTH VULNERABILITY AND EXPOSURE

The four risk terrain models presented above articulate spatial vulnerabilities of places that are most likely to result in "all batteries/assaults," "battery/assault with a firearm," "battery with a weapon," or "battery with serious injury" in the City of Chicago. As determined by the previously discussed Nearest Neighbor (NN) analyses, all

991 battery/assault incidents against police officers cluster spatially. Eleven specific features of the landscape help to create behavior settings for these incidents to occur and cluster. Incidents of battery/assault with a firearm against police officers do not cluster spatially. Yet, there are at least three spatial features common to the settings where these otherwise "randomly" patterned incidents happen. Incidents of battery with a weapon against police officers cluster spatially. Five specific features of the landscape help to create behavior settings for these incidents to occur and cluster. Incidents of serious injury from battery to police officers do not cluster spatially. Yet, there is at least one spatial feature common to the settings where this "dispersed" pattern of incidents occurs.

We now have two valuable pieces of spatial intelligence. First, some categories or outcomes of battery/assault to police officers do not cluster in statistically significant ways. So, a conventional hot spot map of batteries/assaults calculated from a recent past time period to identify existing problematic areas or to suggest areas where battery/assault could occur in the future would not be a viable risk assessment method in all circumstances. Nor is it preferable to have to depend on past battery/assault incidents *and* a continual stream of new (future) incidents in order to assess current risky places for officers when handling calls-for-service. Ideally, police commanders would want to prevent all of these incidents from occurring in the first place. It is not unreasonable to believe that battery/assault to police officers, specifically, could approach zero with proper tactical responses to certain situations (Compton et al., 2014; Compton et al., 2009).

Second, while unique spatial risk factors exist, battery/assault to police officers does not always occur at the places with highest relative risk scores, as defined by a risk terrain model. So, to continue our inquiry into the spatial dynamics of this crime type, we consider the overall effect of risky places as a function of both spatial risks (that is, vulnerabilities) *and* past battery/assault events (that is, exposures). That is, places near where past battery/assault incidents occurred or clustered should strengthen risk assessments of places where police officer battery/assault is most likely to occur. To test this possibility, the risk terrain model for "all batteries/assaults"[5] in 2012 was added to a GIS where counts of January through June 2012 (Period 1) and July through December 2012 (Period 2) battery/assault incidents were joined to each 426ft grid cell. Relative risk scores and Period 1 (P1) battery/assault incidents should be statistically significant "predictors" of Period 2 (P2) battery/assault incident locations, when controlling for one another.

As shown in table 8, the Incidence-Rate Ratio (IRR) from a Poisson regression suggests that the P2 battery/assault count increases 0.91% for every unit increase of risk at a 426ft cell (that is, a place approximately the size of a street block), when controlling for the number of P1 battery/assault incidents.[6] The mean and standard deviation of relative risk scores are 16.23 and 23.74, respectively. So, when controlling for recent past battery/assault incidents at the same place, a cell with a relative risk score above the mean has more than a 14% increased likelihood of experiencing batteries/assaults (0.91 * 16.23). Places with risk scores one standard deviation above the mean have more than a 36% increased likelihood of experiencing battery/assault (0.91 * [16.23 + 23.74]). Places two

TABLE 8   Poisson Regression Results for Relative Risk Score and P1 Battery/
Assault on P2 Battery/Assault, 2012

Variable	IRR	Std. Err.	Z	95% C.I. Lower	95% C.I. Upper
Relative Risk Score (1–582.5)	1.0091*	.00058	15.64	1.00801	1.01031
Battery/Assault Count, P1	2.9844*	.12201	26.74	2.75459	3.23340

*p<0.001

standard deviations above the mean have nearly a 58% increased likelihood of experiencing battery/assault (0.91 * 63.71). Furthermore, a place that experienced a battery/assault within the six months of Period 1 has nearly twice the likelihood of hosting another similar incident during Period 2 (IRR = 2.98), when controlling for relative risk score. These probabilities are statistically significant.

The average relative risk score was multiplied by the IRR to get a percent-likelihood of risk for each place, when controlling for prior incidents. This microlevel map is shown in figure 7. The highest-risk cells—symbolized in red—are where police officers have a nearly 58% or greater likelihood of experiencing battery/assault compared to police officers managing calls-for-service at some other locations.

So, it seems that places with high relative risk scores and where battery/assault incidents have already occurred in the recent past are behavior settings that present exceptionally strong likelihoods of battery/assault to police who handle calls-for-service at these locations. While this general knowledge about *all* batteries/assaults might not apply to some categories that do not cluster, such as "battery resulting in serious injury" or "battery/assault with a firearm," it provides a grounded understanding of the spatial dynamics of battery/assault incidents in Chicago. But a qualification of the practical application of these microlevel results is that addressing risks of battery/assault to Chicago's nearly 12,000 sworn police officers and then allocating resources accordingly to the approximately one-block-sized place unit is difficult within a jurisdiction of 234 square miles. Problem-solving initiatives within the CPD are implemented at the more macro level of police beats. So, to allow for a strategic assessment of risk, the relative risk scores of cells within the risk terrain map of battery/assault were spatially joined to a polygon shapefile of police beats. Spatial risk for each police beat was calculated based on the average relative risk score of cells of the risk terrain map that intersected each beat. Period 1 and Period 2 counts of battery/assault were joined to each beat as well.

As shown in table 9, the IRR from a negative binomial regression[7] suggests that the P2 battery/assault count increases 1.40% for every unit increase of average relative risk at a police beat, when controlling for the number of P1 battery/assault incidents. The mean and standard deviation of risk values are 24.19 and 15.68, respectively. So, when controlling for recent past battery/assault incidents within the same area, a beat with an

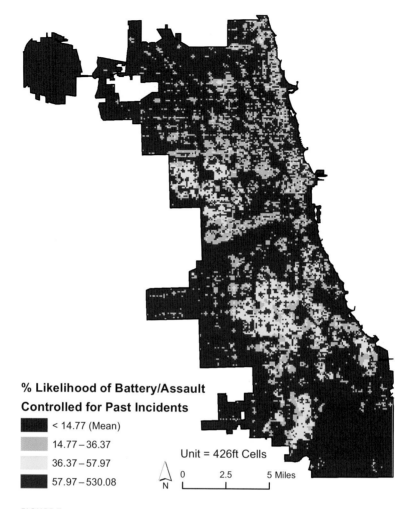

% Likelihood of Battery/Assault Controlled for Past Incidents

- < 14.77 (Mean)
- 14.77 – 36.37
- 36.37 – 57.97
- 57.97 – 530.08

Unit = 426ft Cells

0   2.5   5 Miles

N

FIGURE 7

Microlevel risk terrain map for battery/assault against police officers in Chicago, Illinois.

TABLE 9   Negative Binomial Regression Results for Relative Risk Score and P1 Battery/Assault on P2 Battery/Assault, 2012, at the Police Beat Unit of Analysis

Variable	IRR	Std. Err.	Z	95% C.I. Lower	95% C.I. Upper
Avg. Relative Risk Score (0.92–92.73)	1.01402*	.00340	4.14	1.00736	1.02072
Battery/Assault Count, P1	1.2077*	.03294	6.92	1.14481	1.27403

*p<0.001

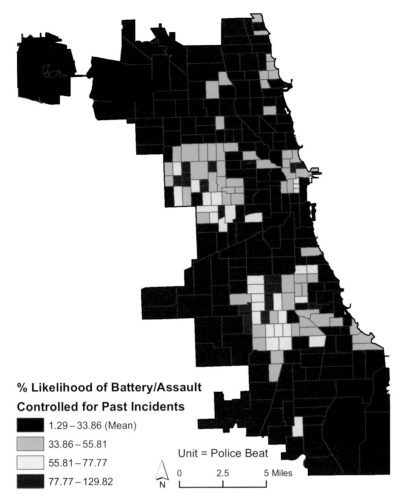

**% Likelihood of Battery/Assault
Controlled for Past Incidents**

■	1.29 – 33.86 (Mean)
▨	33.86 – 55.81
☐	55.81 – 77.77
■	77.77 – 129.82

Unit = Police Beat

0   2.5   5 Miles

N

FIGURE 8

Macrolevel risk terrain map for battery/assault against police officers in Chicago, Illinois.

average relative risk score above the mean has more than a 33% increased likelihood of experiencing battery/assault (1.40 * 24.19). Beats with risk values two standard deviations above the mean have nearly 78% increased likelihood of experiencing battery/assault (1.40 * [24.19 + (2*15.68)]). Furthermore, with each new battery/assault that occurs within a beat, the likelihood of another similar incident occurring within the next six months increases by over 20% (IRR = 1.2077), when controlling for average relative risk score. These probabilities are statistically significant.

The average relative risk score was multiplied by the IRR to get a percent-likelihood of risk for each beat. This macrolevel map is shown in figure 8. The highest-risk beats—symbolized in red—are where CPD officers who work there have a 77% or greater likelihood of experiencing battery/assault compared to police officers working some other beats. With officer safety as one broad-based goal of the CPD, this spatial intel can be used to strategically allocate resources and reform policies and protocols at the macro level of the Chicago police jurisdiction.

EVENT CONTEXT: CASE FILE REVIEW

Microlevel assessments of places within police beats can be made for tactical purposes on a call-by-call basis, particularly when the call-for-service locations are high-risk. Spatial vulnerabilities and exposures, then, are considered within the context of what is known about the events. For instance, precipitators or characteristics of the officer and offender could further influence the risk of battery/assault to police officers (for example, Wortley, 2008; Bohrer, Davis, & Garrity, 2000; Brandl & Stroshine, 2003; Edwards, 1995; Ellis, Choi, & Blaus, 1993; Kaminsky & Sorenson, 1995; Kaminsky, Rojek, Smith, & Alpert, 2012; Kercher, Swedler, Pollack, & Webster, 2013; Tiesman, Hendricks, Bell, & Amandus, 2010). A review of the facts and conditions connected with these types of events elucidates patterns that inform tactical actions above and beyond consideration of geospatial qualities of risk.

General empirical inquiry has quantified some of the influences of situational and person-related risk factors on the likelihood of police officer injury and death. From 1993 to 2012 the average age of officers feloniously killed ranged from 36 to 38 with 10 to 12 years of service (FBI, 2012; Ford, 2000). Younger officers with less training are at greatest risk of injury (Ford, 2000; Kaminsky & Sorenson, 1995). Rabe-Hemp & Schuck (2007) studied violence toward law enforcement in six urban cities and suggested that the effect of gender on battery/assault is conditioned on specific factors of the encounter. Women were more likely to be battered/assaulted when responding to a domestic disturbance call and when the offender was intoxicated. Overall, however, male and female officers did not differ in risk of victimization while on duty (Rabe-Hemp & Schuck, 2007). Studies have also found that officers are more likely to be killed and battered/assaulted in one-officer vehicles than on foot patrol, during undercover work, in two-officer vehicles, on special assignments, or while off-duty (Tucker-Gail, Selman, Kobolt, & Hill, 2010.) In 2012, 64% of battered/assaulted officers were performing duties under the assignment to a one-officer vehicle (FBI, 2012).

These variables could mediate the risks posed by physical features of the landscape. So, in collaboration with Officer Joseph Candella and the Chicago Police Department, case file reviews of the incidents of battery with serious injury that occurred in 2012 were performed to understand the contexts of these aggressive behaviors against Chicago police officers. This category of battery was selected for further study because it did not spatially cluster, leading us to want to know more about these particular events within the contexts of what we already knew about spatial vulnerability.[8]

Psychological theory, specifically environmental psychology,[9] suggests that situationally induced emotional arousal can provoke a criminal response. According to the environmental stress model (Baum, Singer, & Baum, 1981), people under stress respond in ways to manage or adapt to the aversive conditions and events. This is the so-called fight or flight response. Responses to environmental stressors may be physiological (for example, increased adrenaline), emotional (for example, irritability, anxiety) and behavioral (for example, aggression). Basically, certain events at particular places in Chicago could create stress and provoke an antisocial response, such as aggression, because these locations are especially conducive to aggressive behavior toward police (Wortley, 2008). Both environmental and situational cues can prompt this criminal behavior (Smit, van der Vecht, & Lebesque, 2014). So, while spatial risks defined as a function of vulnerability and exposure help to anticipate how crime will be distributed in an area, event context helps to determine the potential level of crime in an area. As Wortley explained in the case of Jim, the function of situational precipitators is to initiate behavior; the immediate environment need only enable the performance of the behavior. In our Chicago case file review, we sought to identify key precipitators that could supply or intensify the motivation for individuals to commit crimes that injured police officers (Wortley, 2001, 2002, 2008). The quality of certain places may be perceived by offenders to be opportune locations (Cohen, Kluegel, & Land, 1981) to behave aggressively toward police. With Officer Candella's research support, we learned important details that advanced our understanding of the spatial dynamics of battery/assault to police.

The case file review focused on several facets of the crime of battery to police with serious injury that were particular to the Chicago jurisdiction (for example, What was the predominant call type? How did the officer respond? Was the event inside or outside problem buildings?). We learned that of all the battery events where officers sustained serious injury in 2012, only two were initially dispatched as "violent" calls. Most originated as nonviolent events. Domestic disturbances accounted for only 19% of the incidents; 33% were pedestrian stops or traffic stops initiated by the officer. Most batteries (85%) occurred against uniformed officers. All offenders were the original subjects of the initial police interaction, so there was no "surprise" as to who the threat might be. Nearly 60% of incidents occurred between 3 PM and 11 PM; 63% of incidents occurred outside of buildings (that is, "on the street"). When battery incidents occurred within close proximity to high concentrations of "problem buildings," the offender tended to live nearby (that is, less than one mile away). This is also notable because the risk terrain model determined that the optimal spatial influence of the solitary risk factor "problem buildings" was "density," with a bandwidth of two blocks. CPD officials surmised that when suspects are familiar with the area and have intimate knowledge of the problem buildings in advance, they are more likely to flee toward them or fight near concentrated areas of them. This understanding of the mechanisms through which problem buildings present risks to police officers is supported by psychological theory and empirical research pertaining to locations that afford suspects with opportunities to elicit assistance from others in evasion or attack. The process of gaining this deduced knowledge is also encouraged by long-established principles of problem-oriented policing (Braga, 2004; Mastrofski, Weisburd, & Braga, 2010).

7

RISK MANAGEMENT
AND RTM IN ACTION

In our various collaborations with researcher and practitioner stakeholders throughout the world, we learned how risk terrain modeling produces customized information products that provide direct decision support for place-based interventions. We also realized from multicity projects that the spatial dynamics of crime are not the same in different settings, even for similar crime types. Standard patterns of crime cannot be expected across study settings (Jacobs, 1961/1992). Think about this through the analogy of a kaleidoscope, first introduced by Kennedy in 1983. The kaleidoscope itself represents the particular environment, or study setting, that we are interested in examining (see figure 9). The pieces of the kaleidoscope (that is, the glass and the cylinder) are similar from one time to another. The mechanisms for bringing the pieces together in certain patterns (for example, gravity, the roundness of the cylinder) operate constantly, and the characteristics of the pieces (color, value) are the same from one turn to another. The patterns that are formed, however, change with different combinations of the pieces. So, it is with crime locations that the shards of glass represent features of that environment, such as bars, fast food restaurants, grocery stores, and the like, that could attract illegal behavior and create spatial vulnerabilities. Moving from study setting to study setting represents a turn of the kaleidoscope whereby the pieces come together in different ways, creating unique spatial and situational contexts that have implications for behavior at those places.

Table 10 presents discrete risk terrain models for robberies in three urban environments: Newark, New Jersey; Chicago, Illinois; and Kansas City, Missouri. The models

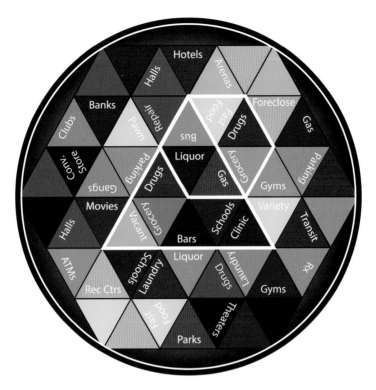

FIGURE 9

The crime risk kaleidoscope illustrates how unique settings for illegal behavior form within or across jurisdictions as pieces come together in different ways, creating unique spatial and situational contexts for crime, as depicted by the triangular or hexagonal outlines in the figure.

were completed in collaboration with our colleague Jeremy Barnum and were produced using the same "pool" of risk factors (for empirical testing) that were common to all three settings. Use your mind's eye to imagine the fact that robbery tends to cluster in certain areas within each city. When we diagnose the underlying characteristics of these "hot spot" areas, we realize that the characteristics of places where these crime incidents are occurring in each city are very different.

Consider the risk factor of *foreclosures,* for instance. While foreclosed properties (as well as being within certain proximity of them) are a significant risk factor across all cities, the relative risk values (that is, weight) and spatial influences of this factor vary greatly within respective models. In Newark and Chicago, it tops the list and carries the greatest weight. In Kansas City, it is relatively less important than the spatial influence of other features of the landscape. Look at the *bars* risk factor in table 10. Bars are commonly associated with violent behavior, but not significantly associated with the spatial contexts for robbery in Kansas City. *Drug markets,* on the other hand, seem to be heavily influencing robberies in Kansas City, yet carry less weight in Chicago and Newark. We

TABLE 10   Risk Terrain Models for Robberies in Three Cities

Risk Factor	Chicago				Kansas City				Newark			
	C	O	SI	RRV	C	O	SI	RRV	C	O	SI	RRV
Foreclosures	4.51	P	852	4.51	0.52	P	1386	1.68	2.26	P	1356	9.61
Gas Stations	1.53	P	213	4.60	0.75	D	462	2.11	0.96	P	226	2.65
Grocery Stores	0.45	P	1065	1.57	0.55	P	1386	1.73	0.39	D	1356	1.47
Health Centers & Gyms	–	–	–	–	–	–	–	–	–	–	–	–
Laundromats	0.82	P	213	2.27	–	–	–	–	1.06	P	226	2.89
Parking Stations	0.67	P	213	1.96	–	–	–	–	0.43	P	904	1.53
Variety Stores	0.23	P	1278	1.25	0.50	D	1386	1.64	–	–	–	–
Bus Stops	0.94	D	426	2.55	1.68	D	1155	5.38	1.30	P	226	3.68
Bars	0.60	P	213	1.83	–	–	–	–	0.38	P	678	1.46
Drug Markets	2.36	D	1065	2.36	2.16	D	231	8.69	0.87	D	226	2.39
Schools	0.32	P	1278	1.39	–	–	–	–	0.45	P	1356	1.57
Parks	–	–	–	–	0.45	P	1386	1.57	–	–	–	–
Liquor Stores	1.09	P	213	2.97	0.78	P	1386	2.19	0.41	P	1356	1.50
Pawn Shops	0.26	P	1278	1.29	–	–	–	–	–	–	–	–
Intercept	-4.56	–	–	–	-6.16	–	–	–	-4.99	–	–	–
Intercept	-0.58	–	–	–	-1.10	–	–	–	-0.84	–	–	–

ABBREVIATIONS: C: Coefficient; O: Operationalization (P=Proximity, D=Density); SI: Spatial Influence (in Feet); RRV: Relative Risk Value asked Sergeant Jonas Baughman of the Kansas City Police Department (KCPD), supervisor of the real-time crime center, to ground-truth the unexpected result regarding bars. He explained that the exclusion of bars as a spatial correlate of robberies makes sense, based on his professional experience. While robberies do occasionally happen near bars, the majority of robberies are not connected to bars regarding their event context. Baughman's event analysis revealed that the victims or offenders of robbery incidents were not reported to be coming from, going to, or presently at a bar around the time of the robbery. There are a small handful of areas with high concentrations of bars in Kansas City, explained Baughman. But, generally, the city does not have a large number of bars despite its large size. Bars that exist are relatively isolated throughout the 314-square-mile landscape of the city, minimizing their spatial significance. The RTM result, he concluded, makes sense.

As evidenced by this three-city comparison, even though crime problems can cluster within cities, the ways in which features of a landscape come together to create unique behavior settings for crime are not necessarily generalizable across cities. Since we are mindful of the kaleidoscope metaphor, it is not safe to assume that a "standard" response to crime problems will provide similar returns across all environments. This is true for areas within jurisdictions (Hart & Miethe, 2015; Caplan, Piza, & Kennedy, 2012) and also across jurisdictions. So one crime problem, such as robberies, will not necessarily respond to a one-size-fits-all intervention strategy (even if the strategy worked elsewhere). Behavior settings differ, so interventions need to be tailored accordingly. RTM facilitates this custom analysis of crime problems at various geographic extents.

The integration of RTM methods into police organizations needs to be performed consistently from one instance to another. Datasets and data sources may change, as could analysts, command staff, or other resources. But the application of RTM within a larger agenda of risk management must be reliable throughout multiple iterations, in different settings, by different people, and for different types of outcome events. To achieve consistency in our own applications of RTM across various jurisdictions, we begin by conversing with key stakeholders to isolate the specific problem to be addressed. Crime is often the focus for police agencies, so we begin with identifying a priority crime type (that is, step 1 of RTM, as discussed in chapter 2). Then our assessment of the spatial dynamics of the priority crime type begins not with the statistical tests of RTM, but with an appraisal of the risk narrative as perceived by stakeholders within the jurisdiction. We meet with police officials and other parties to learn how *they* understand the problem and related event contexts. We listen intently, show humility, and ask questions to gain insights that will ground our methods in the nuanced social, cultural, economic, and political atmospheres within which the priority crime is happening.

This grounded approach helps us identify potential threats to construct and content validity (discussed in chapter 2) that could affect analyses and interpretations of results. It helps us begin to identify datasets and connect potential risk factors and their spatial influences to outcome events (that is, with face validity). And it begins the process of

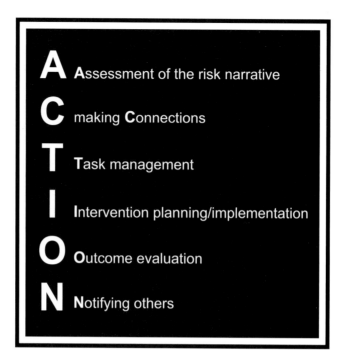

FIGURE 10

Overview of ACTION: a guide for problem solving with a pragmatic focus on Assessment, Connections, Tasks, Interventions, Outcomes, and Notifications to be applied consistently across projects and study settings. ACTION is not necessarily a linear process.

task management, whereby we discuss the feasibility and responsibilities of all parties to perform tasks to collect data and utilize spatial intel, given known constraints and existing strengths of human capital and other resources. Following these initial meetings, we analyze data and produce reports for intervention planning. RTM methods come into play at this point. An intervention planning intel report, or IPIR (discussed below in this chapter), is reviewed with stakeholders in an atmosphere conducive to interpreting results with perspective on event context and the social relevancies of risk factors. Following the planning and implementation of intervention activities, we evaluate outcomes and notify stakeholders and the general public about what was done, why it was done, and the sustainability of efforts used to achieve results.

This pragmatic focus on Assessment, Connections, Tasks, Interventions, Outcomes, and Notifications forms ACTION (figure 10), which we apply consistently across projects and study settings. (For a more detailed discussion of the risk-based approach to crime analysis and the origins of ACTION, see Kennedy & Van Brunschot, 2009.) ACTION is not necessarily a linear process, but rather a guide for applied problem solving whereby each item may be addressed once or iteratively in consequence or concurrently with other items. We have tried several shortcuts to this heuristic over the years, but ultimately realized that meaningful and actionable information from RTM was best achieved within this risk management agenda. Multiple problems require repeated iterations of ACTION.

ASSESSMENT OF THE RISK NARRATIVE

A risk narrative is a spoken or written account of connected events. It is a story, so to speak, about how events, such as crimes, relate to other phenomena in their environments. Assessing the risk narrative is an endeavor to get stakeholders thinking spatially about events and behaviors—beyond only knowledge of victims, offenders, or guardians. The goal in assessing the risk narrative is to identify patterns of behavior and understand how these behaviors engage with the environment and interact with other phenomena to yield specific outcomes. In the policing matrix, Lum (2009) suggests, the most effective strategies for managing crime are those that focus on place. Less effective are policing strategies that solely target offenders.

Underlying the risk narrative is the basic premise that stakeholders engaged in this activity provide information that can be incorporated into spatial intelligence in a way that promotes proactive planning rather than reactive programs. Broadly speaking, an assessment of the risk narrative should characteristically seek to elucidate problems and issues that are high in relevance to the priority crime or related policies, practices, events, and individuals. What is the problem? Who is involved or affected by the problem? How do various stakeholders understand key issues and reconcile contested claims about the problem, its presumed causes, and what should be done to address it? What has already been done to address the problem? How should "success" be defined when future actions are taken to mitigate the problem? And so on.

Crime problems raise questions not just about people's understandings of risk, but about the values and norms informing their identities, perspectives, and preferences (Douglas, 1992). To make risk narratives articulable requires engaging stakeholders with observations and questions about their risk knowledge and the part it plays in social, cultural, and political processes within the study setting (Henwood, Pidgeon, Parkhill, & Simmons, 2010; Henwood, Pidgeon, Sarre, Simmons, & Smith, 2008). Challenging questions need to be posed to stakeholders about ways of conceptualizing and studying risk—not just to gain scientific credibility, but to ensure that the spatial risk analysis and related intervention strategies will be acceptable in the context of police practices and community relations. The risk narrative should value diverse ways of articulating risk, beyond those entailed in established paradigms, practices, or procedures (Henwood et al., 2010).

A risk narrative yields many valuable insights. First, it presents a clear idea of the problem that we are trying to solve. Second, it helps us understand the extent to which we can measure the risk that is posed, and what techniques we should use to operationalize and collect data about the factors that we have identified as important for empirical study. Third, it modestly considers whether or not the factors surmised to correlate with outcome events could be addressed in a feasible intervention that would be attuned to community expectations. This is useful for anticipating the scope of problem-solving efforts, with deference to the likelihood that risk is not constant across time or place, but can vary by time of day, week, or year. Fourth, it begins to define the spatial dimensions of crime. This includes insight into hot spots and cold spots of crime, and how victims, offenders, and other stakeholders use these areas daily: we learn what it takes to keep a location crime-free. Finally, we discover the nature of the police organization itself as a risk-based institution. In addressing crime problems, police consider the safety of their officers and the well-being of the public they serve. Police balance duty to serve with legal liabilities and public relations and perceptions. The best practices of police within this risk balance need to match up to the problem-solving efforts of the intervention, without compromising the police's or the public's concerns.

ASSESSMENT OF THE RISK NARRATIVE

TIMING

At the start of any problem-solving endeavor.

1. A clear statement of what problem is being addressed, where it is located, and the expected consequence of an intervention that is developed to address the problem.

2. Description of past events, with an explanation as to what is known and what may be unknown about the crime problem based on what others have found.

3. Descriptions of populations and environments with expectations about likely outcomes.

4. Inventory of policy steps taken to manage exposure to the problem; account of existing local expenditures directed at or related to the problem.

5. Inventory of existing available resources.

6. Review of existing crime data, hot spots, cold spots, and crime event analyses, and other accessible data sources and information/intelligence products.

MAKING CONNECTIONS

When we study crime patterns with RTM, we want to know what attracts illegal behavior to high-crime areas and why crimes cluster there over time. We study how spatial environments influence criminal behaviors. The charge of making connections for ACTION is to identify factors that might spatially correlate with the priority crime and identify valid and reliable datasets for measures thereof, to develop new collection and management protocols for needed datasets, and to distill probable links between potential risk factors and their spatial influences to outcome events. Connections emanate from the risk narrative.

Research generally is focused on making connections between variables—determining how one factor or a group of factors influence an outcome. In terms of crime, there is extensive literature that has been compiled about relationships between all sorts of factors, be they offender characteristics, victim traits, locational features, or situational opportunities. It is important for risk management endeavors to articulate these connections. In early stages, such as when drafting a risk narrative, this is done through educated guesses, stakeholder insights, and past research. Connections are made in consultation with police, residents, and other stakeholders within the study setting, as well as through reviews of relevant literature, reports, policies, and local media reports. Making connections in the risk narrative helps anticipate what to expect from empirical analysis. In so doing, we can be conscious of the first and fifth requirements of successful forecasting (discussed in chapter 2): ensuring that data used in the analysis are reliable and valid, including both content and construct validities, that the datasets and their sources are sustainable to allow for replication and continued modeling, and that the RTM outputs are within a range of reasonable expectations (that is, face validity).

In the later stages of risk management (for example, the "I" in ACTION), connections are made through statistical analysis and RTM. In building a risk terrain model, we make connections from the point of view of spatial influence. So, early on, be sure to consider the face validity of proximity and density effects of risk factors on crime outcomes. Recall, for example, that KCPD officials do not believe there to be areas in the city with highly concentrated bars. This perception (of irrelevance to "density") is important for researchers to know from the outset of analysis. If the risk analysis produces information that is unlikely or extreme based on past experience or theoretical knowledge, then early stakeholder insights help us understand why the result could have been produced, or else it helps to revise the datasets or other elements of the assessment in a nonarbitrary way. Connections made in the risk narrative set up nuanced insights for researchers to question the face validity of RTM outputs. This aids in judging the degree to which the empirical spatial risk analysis appears reasonable in terms of its stated aims and the many realities of the study setting involved.

Making connections can also be thought of as a ground-truthing endeavor, whereby researchers gather data in the field that either confirms or disputes output results from statistical methods. Do the data actually represent what appears in real life? Existing datasets that are to be used for RTM can be verified, or ground-truthed, to help substantiate or criticize RTM outputs in constructive ways. The risk terrain model for battery with serious injury to police officers in Chicago is an example of this. Upon case file review, the solitary risk factor of "problem buildings" was deemed to have face validity due to the realization that offenders' residences were in close proximity to this factor. Sergeant Baughman provided similar insights regarding bars in Kansas City.

Rather than allowing statistical analyses solely to determine what is selected through a hodgepodge collection of variables, the task of making connections allows us to choose thoughtfully the most theoretically reasonable factors that are expected to impact particular types of crime. Then, if certain factors are empirically selected through RTM, we are able to consider these findings in terms of previously addressed explanations, enabling a validity test to our assessment. When making connections, we are also aware that there is often complexity in relationships, which means that we want not only to know which factors are important in bringing about spatial influence, but also to make a judgment about their relative importance. This last point is essential, as it helps us sort out which factors to focus attention on, not just because they appear to be statistically related to the outcome, but also because they have a relatively great impact on it. Potential risk factors and their spatial influences to illegal behavior should be reified in a risk narrative; but connections should be made without obscuring essential nuanced insights about the social, cultural, and political processes and situational contexts that give risk its meaning to people in their daily lives (Henwood et al., 2010).

MAKING CONNECTIONS

TIMING

During risk narrative; before and after producing a risk terrain model.

1. Connections between spatial features and crime outcomes.
2. Explanations for crime events, and patterns thereof.
3. Hypotheses about crime occurrence.
4. Audits of related successful interventions.
5. Literature reviews.

TASK MANAGEMENT

A key goal of task management is to decide the feasibility and responsibilities for performing tasks to collect data, perform analyses, and respond to information and spatial intelligence, given known constraints and existing strengths of human capital and other resources. Task management should consider who does what with which resources and when. ACTION assumes that stakeholders (or their agencies) will not just collect information about crime problems but also, as part of risk management, prescribe ways in which to address problems. While the analytical function is meant to inform policing operations, inattention to how this should occur disrupts the flow of ideas and articulations of tasks. A risk-based intervention is more than the statistical tests used to inform it, so task management must be embedded in the agency's overall plan. If direct responsibility of the intervention rests with the police department, then command staff must fully understand and be committed to the objectives of the intervention activities and how they are intended to work.

Task management has varied greatly among the agencies we have worked with. There is all too often a divide between the analysts and police leadership in terms of resources and tactics needed to address problems identified through statistical analysis. The consultation and deliberation over appropriate measures to respond to vulnerabilities can challenge the creativity and originality of all parties. In particular, there is a need to consider how certain crime problems can be defined and mitigated through actions that may not appear to be directly associated with the crime event. For example, an educational campaign warning apartment tenants not to warm their cars on cold mornings by running engines with keys in the ignition (what they call "puffers" in Colorado) can be a strategy to reduce motor vehicle theft. But it does not involve the traditional elements of policing, such as setting up bait cars or otherwise arresting thieves in the act. Commitment by leadership goes a long way to starting interventions, but as important is the ongoing participation of all levels of sworn and civilian police personnel in the process of intervention planning, implementation, and outcome evaluation. These tasks cannot be left to the analysts to figure out on their own or to communicate (or dictate) to sworn personnel. This is why a clear set of tasks that can be coordinated from the top of an organization needs to be articulated and managed. Leadership from the top sets priorities, but as importantly, it sets the tone and culture of risk-based policing with a focus on assessment and management. Within policing organizations, task management may involve sorting out the responsibilities of officers on patrol, the decisions made by supervisors about how implementation strategies are developed, or the priorities that are set to meet the challenges of the intervention activities. As exemplified with the educational campaign to address motor vehicle thefts (discussed above), task management may also involve thinking about the job to be done in different ways than before.

In Colorado Springs, Colorado, where motor vehicle thefts were the priority crime type, police leadership decided that noise complaint calls, which were identified as spatial precipitators to motor vehicle thefts, should get higher priority for response. The drastic change mandated a response time of approximately three minutes instead of the previous average of many hours. This required a new set of tasks to be set for dispatchers to meet this mandate. When these instructions were received, someone needed to follow up to make sure the plan was implemented properly. Task management cannot be taken for granted and needs to be clearly sorted out at the beginning of intervention planning.

TASK MANAGEMENT

TIMING

Prior to intervention planning; ongoing.

1. Determine roles to be played by each of the actors in the intervention: that is, analysts, police officers, and so on.

2. Develop time lines for intervention activities and the tasks that need to be completed to achieve deadlines.

3. Coordinate intervention planning, implementation, and evaluation activities, including data collection.

INTERVENTION PLANNING AND IMPLEMENTATION

Key to successful risk management is a sophisticated information gathering and analysis process, one that integrates a variety of analytical techniques and allows insights from each method to inform the use of additional techniques—with a common goal of articulating the spatial dynamics of crime. Police agencies, for years, have suffered from both incomplete and stale information, as well as the absence of procedures for holistically tying sources of data and information together to identify trends, provide leads, and comprehensively understand spatial dynamics of people, behavior, and crime. Furthermore, there are often disconnects between information products and resultant activities. Recall from chapter 4, for instance, how hot spot mapping results in police responses to crime that are inherently offender-focused, not place-based. With the proliferation of data fusion centers and real-time crime centers, the possibility of tying together information sources for intelligence production is greatly enhanced. This infrastructure and these investments in human capital provide a major step forward in identifying crime risks and pursuing risk management. But data without direction are really of no value. Data have to be studied and communicated in a way that informs thoughtful decision making so there is confidence and buy-in to the conclusions that are drawn from analytical products.

Risk terrain modeling can be framed within the context of an intervention planning intel report, or IPIR, in that RTM is a spatial risk analysis technique that informs one's understanding of crime problems by complementing other analytical techniques to paint a comprehensive picture of the spatial dynamics of crime. Our consultation on risk management endeavors often begins after a problem has been identified in an area, such as the matter of battery to police officers in Chicago, or the problems of violence in New York, or motor vehicle theft in Colorado Springs. These problems create risks to people and property, so risk management is called for. ACTION is a component of a risk management agenda that produces spatial knowledge. Within ACTION is the need for intervention planning, which is where RTM fits in: RTM is a fundamental part of the IPIR and resulting evidence-based intervention strategy.

Intervention planning intel reports present spatial analyses to police agencies, and they use these reports to develop interventions. The IPIR can have many parts, but its main purpose is to outline the ways in which the problem under study occurs in the study setting and the factors that are important in elevating risks of it continuing. The IPIR also provides guidance on what the analytical information means, and offers suggestions for steps that can be taken to translate the data analysis into actionable intelligence and defined tactics for intervention. The IPIR is place-based: it identifies locations in which the targeting of the problem will be most effective. But it also prioritizes the risk factors to be addressed relative to their impact on the problem so that resources can be allocated and people can be tasked with what to do about the places when they get there.

Components of an IPIR are discussed below, based on an actual report for our research project in Glendale, Arizona, in collaboration with Eric Piza, funded by National Institute of Justice (NIJ). The purpose of the Glendale IPIR was to inform the design and implementation of risk-based intervention activities to affect the frequencies and spatial distributions of postintervention robbery crime events at places. Data analyzed were current for the calendar year 2012. This IPIR content, including pin mapping, hot spot mapping, near repeat analysis, and RTM, may be considered a template, or these methods can be adapted to meet the needs of a particular project or audience. Additional analytical techniques can be incorporated as well. The key aim should be to integrate insights from a variety of methods to produce a comprehensive understanding of the spatial dynamics of crime. The analyses should progress from descriptive and exploratory toward explanatory data analysis. The final product should provide an empirical basis for a risk narrative that informs intervention strategies in meaningful and actionable ways. Along with the IPIR, we provide stakeholders with all utilized datasets in shapefile and KML (Keyhole Markup Language) formats. This increases the transparency of the report, and permits stakeholders to delve deeper into the data. KML files permit display on Google Earth, which is generally accessible (and user-friendly) to a broad audience.

PIN MAP AND NEAREST NEIGHBOR (CLUSTER) ANALYSIS

The IPIR begins with a pin map of crime data, as shown in figure 11. Visual inspection of the points in the map suggests that crimes are not uniformly distributed throughout the jurisdiction and may be clustered at certain areas. Results of the Nearest Neighbor (NN) analysis for spatial randomness suggest that the distribution of crimes is significantly clustered (Obs. Mean Dist. = 178.36; Exp. Mean Dist. = 968.16; NN Ratio = 0.18; Z-score = -39.14; $p<0.001$).

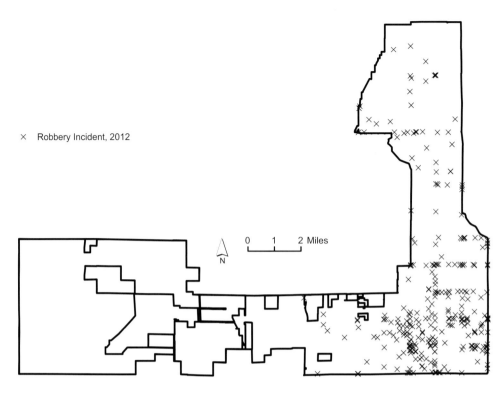

FIGURE 11
Pin map of robberies in Glendale, Arizona.

KERNEL DENSITY MAPS

Kernel density mapping serves as a useful follow-up to visual reviews of pin maps and NN analysis because it shows where the highest concentrations of crime incidents are occurring at more localized places within the study area. Figure 12 is a density map of robberies in Glendale. The density map is symbolized according to standard deviational breaks, with all places colored in black having density values greater than two standard deviations above the mean density value. The kernel density map suggests that there are several hot spot areas for crime in the jurisdiction. Inquiry into crime clusters may be continued with any number of well-established techniques to verify statistically significant hot spot areas (Drawve, 2014; Eck, Chainey, Cameron, Leitner, & Wilson, 2005; Chainey, Tompson, & Uhlig, 2008; Van Patten, McKeldin-Coner, & Cox, 2009).

SPATIAL STABILITY ANALYSIS

Table 11 presents results from a Chi-Squared Test of kernel density hot spots during each quarter of 2012. In the 236ft by 236ft places in the hot spot areas, about half of subsequent (that is, next quarter) crime incidents occurred within these same places. This

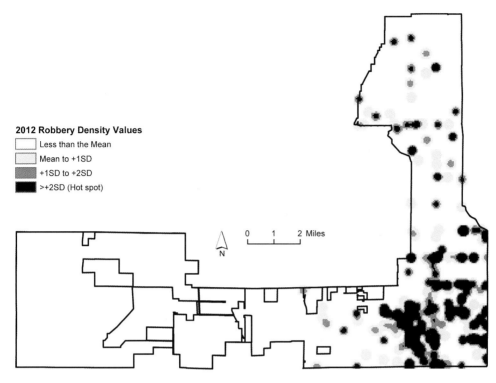

2012 Robbery Density Values
☐ Less than the Mean
▨ Mean to +1SD
▨ +1SD to +2SD
■ >+2SD (Hot spot)

0   1   2 Miles

N

FIGURE 12

Density map of robberies in Glendale, Arizona.

TABLE 11   Chi-Squared Test of Hot Spot Prediction

	% of cells with any crimes during the following quarter	Hot spot area accounts for this % of jurisdiction	% of places within hot spot area that hosts any future crimes
Q1 Hot spot	45.0*	7.0	1.4
Q2 Hot spot	50.6*	7.6	1.2
Q3 Hot spot	54.7*	7.9	1.4

*p<0.01

means that half of future crime events did not occur at recent-past hot spot areas. Robberies do not always occur in the future where they often did in the past. According to table 11, relatively few places within larger hot spot areas account for the new crime incident locations. For instance, Q1 hot spots covered 7% of the jurisdiction's area, but only 1.4% of the places within the hot spot areas hosted any Q2 crimes. This suggests that something more than hot spots of recent-past crimes are attracting new criminal behavior at places.

The Theory of Risky Places proposes that if a crime occurs in a high-risk location, the chances of a future crime occurring nearby increase. So, the examination of near repeats can enhance the picture of crime occurrence and help to better focus strategies for place-based interventions. The daily expected robbery crime count (DECC) in Glendale is 1.72, based on the number of crimes that happened in the calendar year 2012 (N = 935), divided by 365 days. The DECC helps to estimate resources that may be needed for the intervention so that activities can be temporarily targeted at new crime locations that have a high propensity for attracting near repeat incidents (as discussed in chapter 5). If we take into account the DECC and available resources, priority attention could be given to high-risk places in the target area that are within 357 feet (that is, the expected near repeat bandwidth)[1] from each new crime incident for a fixed period of time.

A review of temporal heat maps, such as figure 13, can inform the production of temporally constrained risk terrain models that isolate the risk factors attracting criminal behavior at peak days or time periods. For instance, risk terrain models can be produced for the crime-dense periods of "Monday thru Thursday, from 6 to 10 PM" or "Friday thru Sunday, 5 PM to midnight." This spatial-temporal intelligence fuels stakeholder discussions about the event contexts of crimes nearby to key risk factors to make connections that advance the risk narrative.

RISK TERRAIN MODELING AND HIGH-RISK CLUSTER ANALYSIS

RTM helps to diagnose why crimes have already clustered at certain places and to forecast where crimes are likely to emerge in the future. Three separate risk terrain models were produced for robbery in Glendale, in accordance with the steps outlined in chapter 2: a Calendar Year (CY) 2012 model (n = 629 robberies); a CY Weekday model (n = 351); and a CY Weekend model (n = 282). The spatial influences of 11 potential risk factors were considered: bars, liquor stores, restaurants with liquor licenses, drug calls-for-service, apartment complexes, parks, gang member residences, convenience stores, take-out restaurants, automated teller machines (ATMs), and gas stations. All geographic calculations were conducted using raster cells of 236 feet (N = 31,197) and an average block length of 472 feet.

A risk terrain model for CY robberies contains seven risk factors. Beginning with the most influential: drug calls-for-service (Density, 236ft, RRV = 15.56), convenience stores (Proximity, 472ft, RRV = 2.88), take-out restaurants (Proximity, 472ft, RRV = 2.54), apartments (Proximity, 1416ft, RRV = 2.53), gang member residences (Density, 708ft, RRV = 2.41), liquor stores (Density, 1416ft, RRV = 2.30), and bars (Proximity, 472ft, RRV = 2.19). The risk terrain map has relative risk scores for each place ranging from 1 for the lowest-risk place to 1605.8 for the highest-risk place (Mean = 3.01; SD = 27.45).

Hr/Day	M	Tu	W	Th	F	Sa	Su
0	0	0	0	0	0	0	0
1	7	1	2	2	6	3	7
2	10	0	2	4	14	4	10
3	0	6	0	0	6	18	6
4	28	16	8	8	8	12	8
5	5	0	5	0	15	0	0
6	0	0	6	0	0	6	0
7	7	7	28	7	14	7	0
8	48	48	0	16	16	40	0
9	0	0	27	27	0	0	27
10	40	10	10	50	0	10	10
11	33	11	55	11	11	11	33
12	48	24	24	36	48	36	24
13	0	52	52	117	13	78	104
14	42	70	28	14	0	28	98
15	0	45	60	75	75	0	105
16	32	80	128	112	16	0	96
17	51	34	102	85	187	119	204
18	90	162	90	108	0	126	18
19	76	209	152	247	38	133	114
20	120	160	180	160	100	60	80
21	147	84	126	126	231	84	126
22	440	22	88	220	132	264	132
23	161	23	92	0	253	92	115

FIGURE 13

Temporal heat map showing that 2012 robbery crimes in Glendale, Arizona, cluster by time of day and week.

A risk terrain model for CY Weekday robberies (that is, those that occurred on Monday through Thursday) contains six risk factors. Beginning with the most influential: drug calls-for-service (Density, 236ft, RRV = 12.16), ATMs (Proximity, 472ft, RRV = 4.04), liquor stores (Proximity, 944ft, RRV = 3.45), gang member residences (Density, 708ft, RRV = 2.78), apartments (Proximity, 236ft, RRV = 2.56), and take-out restaurants (Proximity, 1416ft, RRV = 2.05). The risk terrain map has relative risk scores for each place ranging from 1 to 2491.5 (Mean = 2.47; SD = 26.02).

A risk terrain model for CY Weekend robberies (that is, those that occurred on Friday through Sunday) has five risk factors. Beginning with the most influential: drug calls-for-service (Density, 236ft, RRV = 19.87), gas stations (Proximity, 236ft, RRV = 8.18), liquor stores (Density, 708ft, RRV = 3.82), apartments (Proximity, 1180ft, RRV = 3.71), and convenience stores (Proximity, 472ft, RRV = 2.99). The risk terrain map has relative risk scores for each place ranging from 1 to 2307.4 (Mean = 2.65; SD = 28.74).

A Getis-Ord Gi* statistic (Z score) for each place in the three respective risk terrain maps was calculated in a GIS. Results suggest that there are many statistically significant high-risk clusters of places for robbery in Glendale. Results also show that spatial risks cluster differently on weekdays compared to weekends. (See figure 14.) This pattern is statistically significant.

JOINT UTILITY OF VULNERABILITY AND EXPOSURES

As presented in tables 12 to 14, each increased unit of risk at a place raises the likelihood of a crime occurring at that place. In Glendale, robberies are very likely to emerge at high-risk places. But further, the odds of robberies occurring at high-risk places more than doubles with each new recent-past crime incident, when controlling for relative risk scores. The range of relative risk scores for this risk terrain model is 1–1605.8. So, based on the observed Odds Ratio in table 12, places with a risk score two standard deviations above the mean have a 23% (0.4 × 57.9) increased likelihood of experiencing robbery. Higher-risk places are significantly likely to experience crime, particularly those high-risk places located within known hot spot areas.

POWER ANALYSIS AND TARGET AREA SELECTION

What does power have to do with target area selection? Power refers to the probability that a statistical test will detect a crime reduction produced by the intervention, particularly by generating a statistically significant result. Statistical power is used here to inform the optimal size (of the target areas) and duration of the targeted intervention. Generally speaking, a low-powered test has a heightened risk of generating a "false negative." An example of a "false negative" could be a blood test not detecting the presence of a disease in a patient when in fact a disease is present. With respect to a risk-based intervention, a false negative would be the evaluation determining that the intervention did not have a significant effect on crime when it really did. Glendale's evaluation of the intervention incorporated two separate tests: an independent samples t-test and a more rigorous negative binomial regression analysis. Since power analyses are test-specific, power estimates were conducted separately for these tests, with desired statistical value set to 0.8.

A power analysis suggests that place sample sizes of 42 (21 Targeted), 102 (51 Targeted), and 620 (310 Targeted) would be necessary for the t-tests to detect large, medium, and small intervention effects, respectively.[2] In each case, half of the sample should be designated as target areas for the intervention with the others serving as the control areas. According to the power analysis for the negative binomial regression models, the necessary number of crime incidents in the target areas (across the pre- and during-intervention periods) to achieve a power of at least 0.8 with at least a 30% crime

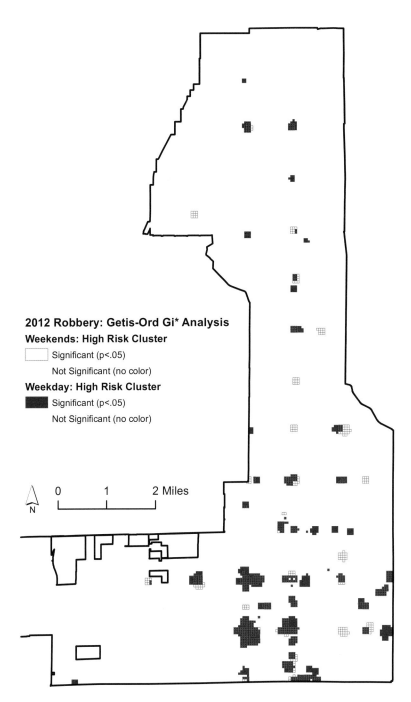

FIGURE 14

Comparison of weekday and weekend risk clusters for robbery a section of Glendale, Arizona.

TABLE 12   Vulnerability-Exposure Logistic Regression on 2012 Q2 Robbery

Variable	B	S.E.	Wald	df	Sig.	Odds Ratio
Relative Risk Score	.004	.001	36.194	1	<0.001	1.004
Q1 Robbery Count	1.579	.168	88.740	1	<0.001	4.850

n = 46,612

TABLE 13   Vulnerability-Exposure Logistic Regression on 2012 Q3 Robbery

Variable	B	S.E.	Wald	df	Sig.	Odds Ratio
Relative Risk Score	.004	.001	27.805	1	<0.001	1.004
Q2 Robbery Count	1.648	.145	128.415	1	<0.001	5.197

n = 46,612

TABLE 14   Vulnerability-Exposure Logistic Regression on 2012 Q4 Robbery

Variable	B	S.E.	Wald	df	Sig.	Odds Ratio
Relative Risk Score	.005	.001	63.365	1	<0.001	1.005
Q3 Robbery Count	1.684	.159	112.259	1	<0.001	5.388

n = 46,612

reduction is 117 incidents. So, the duration of the intervention should be long enough to expect this many incidents in the targeted areas under "normal" circumstances.

Using the aforementioned analyses of the spatial nature and distribution of robbery crimes in the jurisdiction, we recommended to police the following guidelines for target area selection: (1) select places with higher-risk values; (2) give priority to hot spot areas containing a high proportion of high-risk places; (3) include high-risk places that are outside of, but nearby, hot spot areas.

INTERVENTION STRATEGY GUIDELINES

Risk-based interventions should include at least three simultaneous activities[3]—at least one that relates to each of the following categories:

1. Reducing the spatial influence of one or more environmental risk factors.
    a. The risk factors that were empirically selected and included in the risk terrain models are what should receive focused attention for purposes of mitigation efforts, with priority given to factors in order of their weighted influence.

2. Developing evidence-based practices, such as activities related to target-hardening, situational prevention, and community awareness.

3. Using policing activities and patrols to deter and incapacitate known or motivated offenders.

We further recommended the integration of tactical intervention activities that are routinely informed by dynamic crime analysis for the purpose of resource allocations at places within the established target areas. For instance, each new crime incident that locates within the target areas could be evaluated for its propensity to become an instigator for near repeats based on the proportion of high-risk places within the expected near repeat bandwidth. Task managers can then prioritize place-based deployments of resources at the micro level within the target areas by comparing new crime incidents relative to all others according to the surrounding environment's suitability for hosting new near repeat incidents. Priority attention can temporarily be given—and limited resources (re)allocated—to crime incident locations that have more high-risk "slices of the pie" than other incident locations.

OPERATIONALIZING THE IPIR

The IPIR presents a structured evidence-based analysis of the spatial dynamics of the problem at hand. This permits informed decision making during the planning and implementation stages of interventions. Upon completion of an IPIR, we renew conversations with police department officials and other stakeholders to advance the risk narrative, ground-truth connections between variables that were made by the risk terrain model, schedule intervention start and end dates, and formalize the management of tasks. During these meetings with key stakeholders and task managers, which tend to last anywhere from four to six hours, we select target areas for the intervention and steer thinking toward a risk-based approach to intervention activities, with an end-of-meeting goal to operationalize the IPIR content with strategies and tactics for actions consistent with the spatial intelligence presented in the IPIR.

For each risk factor identified in the risk terrain model, we ask stakeholders to explain how they understand its relationship to the priority crime. What are the likely mechanisms at play that link the risk factor to the priority crime? For example, a key risk factor for robbery in Glendale was "convenience stores." Through our inquiry and subsequent discussion about this factor, Glendale police officials explained how most robberies resulted in the theft of cell phones, and that many convenience stores in the city have self-service kiosks to recycle or sell used mobile devices (such as phones) for instant cash payment. They surmised that this explained the spatial correlation (that is, the connection) between the "convenience store" risk factor and the close proximity of robbery incidents. That is, convenience stores (and the kiosks within) provided a quick and nearby method for disposing of stolen goods for instant cash—oftentimes, even before the victim could find a way to notify police about the crime.

After connections are made between factors in the risk terrain model and the priority crime, we ask stakeholders to prioritize the risk factors that should receive focused attention—given available resources and their understanding of how the risk factors are related to the crime problem. Priority is often given in order of relative risk values, but that is not a requirement. Stakeholders are encouraged to select some or all of the risk factors whose spatial influences they believe have the greatest potential for mitigation.

Once factors are selected to receive focused attention, the group proposes actions that police and other stakeholders can take to mitigate the spatial influences of these risk factors. Ultimately, these will be the activities that will occur as part of the intervention. Multiple activities may be performed to address a single risk factor: all appropriate options are considered. Referring back to the "convenience store" risk factor for robbery in Glendale, one method of risk mitigation proposed was to speak to the place managers of convenience stores and encourage them to locate the kiosks near the front of the store and to remove or reduce the signage from the storefront windows in order to make it easier for people outside to see in. This could be especially valuable for police after a BOLO (Be on the Look-Out) is issued for robbery suspects. Increased visibility from the street may mitigate the spatial influence of convenience stores by making them less attractive locations to dispose of stolen goods because of the increased ease with which the premises can be surveilled.

SEVEN PRINCIPLES FOR IMPLEMENTING RISK-BASED INTERVENTIONS

Analytical techniques utilized in the IPIR should comply with the minimum requirements for successful forecasting, as discussed in chapter 2. Furthermore, as the content of the IPIR is brokered for operations and intervention planning, seven principles should be considered.

First, have clearly defined target areas that are distinctly identified as high-risk. Veering away from these areas is fine in pursuit of crime, but this should be the exception, not the rule.

Second, risk factors in the target area should be clearly identified so the intervention can focus on these risks; the intervention should not just be a concentration of effort around hot spots of crime. Let the IPIR inform strategies that tell police what to do when they get to the target areas, not just where to go. The goal should be more than offender-focused law enforcement practices; include efforts to mitigate spatial influences of risky features for long-term impact.

Third, develop strategies for both action and analysis. With an understanding of the mechanisms for how risk factors may affect nearby crime incidents, you can develop actions to mitigate them. But this principle is also a reminder to consider multiple data sources and assessment methods for operational planning and evaluation. Risk is dynamic. The very presence of police in an area changes the risk calculation for both motivated offenders and potential victims. The initial problem analysis that informed the intervention strategy does not have to be the final one. Utilize analysts to consider opportunities for tactical applications of intervention strategies—for example, at specific times or particular places within the target areas.[4] Pull intel from a variety of sources to interpret the relevance of risk factors at risky places and at certain times, and to consider the potential that different policing actions can have the best effects in some places, but not others, depending on the nuances of these places and the situational contexts. Although target areas may be static (that is, if target areas don't change for the duration of the intervention period), places within the target areas are very dynamic. Analysts can help inform tactical actions during the intervention that cater to this fact.

Fourth, the collection of data needs to be both valid and reliable. By this we mean that the actions that are done in an area should clearly relate to the intervention strategy directed at specific risks. Also, it is imperative that accurate geolocated measures of these actions are collected to be able to identify where and when the intervention activity occurred. Document the intended spatial influences of intervention activities (for example, What was the intended area of impact for a uniformed foot patrol or a parked patrol car?). This helps with operationalizing activities to a GIS map and allows for evaluations of their impacts that are meaningful (that is, construct/content validities). Intervention activities may affect the spatial dynamics of crime in areas surrounding the vicinity of the activity's recorded location. This may not apply to all intervention activities. But consider how it might, as appropriate.

Fifth, expect that risk factors may become less risky over time. The risk from features of the landscape should abate over time as a result of the intervention. For this to be measurable, a clear accounting of what the intervention actions did to reduce risk should be articulated as part of the plan based on the expected or intended affect of intervention activities. This relates to the aforementioned fourth principle. But it also is a reminder to routinely reassess the meaningfulness of target areas, risk factors, and intervention strategies—they need to change along with the dynamic nature of illegal behavior and crime patterns that are responding to the intervention activities. Remember, intervention activities are "features" of the environment too, and can alter behaviors of people using these spaces. Establish lines of communication with all police personnel (stakeholders) to solicit and receive comments, information, and suggestions regarding emerging crime problems, risk factors, or other issues regarding the target areas, priority crime type, or other relevant aspects of the problem.

Sixth, let the analysis inform the intervention and the intervention results inform subsequent analyses to better the "next round" of intervention activities. One measure of success might be the extent to which there is a diffusion of benefits that appears in areas surrounding target areas. Spatial or temporal lags might result in longer-term impacts to lower-risk places earlier in the intervention period, while higher-risk places may need more time to respond to the point where long-term effects are measurable.

Finally, consider the expected daily crime count and plan intervention lengths accordingly so that you can measure outcomes reliably, and with sufficient power. Statistical power can be affected by the length of the intervention and its geographic scope. You must have sufficient cases in the target areas for a statistically valid evaluation to be performed. Why should police want to know if their impacts are statistically valid? Because they want to be able to repeat the effect next time they respond to a problem. That should be the essence of problem-oriented policing and risk management. If crime counts reduced and you can attribute it directly to your intervention activities, then you not only get the credit for success, but you know what to do next time the problem occurs. If your intervention strategy did not have the desired result, then you have a foundation for improving it next time. Once you get it right, you can repeat it.

INTERVENTION PLANNING AND IMPLEMENTATION

TIMING

After the risk assessment is completed and a risk narrative is clearly articulated.

1. Produce IPIR.
2. Select target areas and develop intervention strategy for implementation.
3. Implement risk reduction activities, consistent with intervention strategy.
4. Collect intervention activities data throughout implementation phase.

OUTCOME EVALUATION

Key to successful risk management is a well-organized information system that provides data about exposure and vulnerability, and also permits an ongoing evaluation of the success of intervention activities. It is sometimes difficult to collect detailed information about police activities beyond arrest or citation data. However, with a clearly articulated set of goals expressed, the required data can be more easily defined and efforts made (that is, through task management) to collect it. The outcome evaluation involves establishing whether or not the intervention that took place actually worked via meeting or exceeding expectations. With risk management, we are not only interested in the state of the crime problem prior to the implementation of an intervention, but concerned as well with the changes that can be attributed to the intervention activities happening in the target areas.

There is extensive literature in many fields, including criminology, of the steps that are needed to evaluate the success or failure of interventions. The most popular measure of success is a crime rate drop. The simple desistance of crime must be supported, however, through systematic observation, careful documentation of change, and comparisons to locations that have received no treatment, controlling the effects of random increases or decreases in criminal activity. Outcome evaluations should not only measure changes in crime counts, but also assess changes in the spatial patterns of crime occurrence (for example, with a new IPIR). Outcomes can also consider diffusion of benefits and assess whether crime displacement occurred (for example, to high-risk places or elsewhere). Ekblom (1999) explains displacement as part of an evolutionary process in which "offenders adapt their methods of attack to circumvent current preventative measures" (p. 28). One consequence of the strategies police choose for risk mitigation may be to "shape" offenders in a particular way that makes them more adaptable or specialized (p. 42). Outcome evaluations, therefore, are needed so police and other stakeholders can, in turn, readjust with fresh intelligence products and intervention strategies.

There should also be an attempt to establish whether or not the proper procedures have been implemented and that these are replicable in future iterations of the intervention. The successes and failures of task management can be addressed through a process evaluation that is completed at the end of the intervention. Whereas outcome evaluations assess the effectiveness of an intervention in producing intended change, process evaluations help stakeholders see how an intervention outcome was achieved (that is, for better or worse). Process evaluations look at the different roles that key actors played and their effectiveness in meeting intervention objectives. Included in this review could be a survey that canvasses key stakeholders about their role in the project and how they believed the work that they did impacted on project goals, as well as suggestions for improved and more effective management of resources. It is important to give feedback to all stakeholders involved in the intervention so they can perceive transparency in repeated iterations of ACTION and their connections to thoughtful modifications of intervention activities or target areas as the spatial dynamics of crimes change. Most people do not "get it right" the first time. So, a successful intervention may be the one that resulted in valuable insights for significantly improving the next iteration. That's why process and outcome evaluations are so important, and why results should be considered within the context of one another.

OUTCOME EVALUATIONS

TIMING

After intervention activities are implemented.

1. Well-documented data sources.
2. Clearly identified target and control areas.
3. Careful and systematic evaluation of processes and outcomes of the intervention.
4. Plan for sustainable resource allocation to maintain positive aspects of the intervention.

Notifying others involves communicating information. An IPIR notifies police about the spatial dynamics of crime. But notification in ACTION requires more. It should utilize technology, media outlets, and personal communications to share key information about risk management efforts with a variety of stakeholder populations. It should open interactions among civilian and sworn personnel, analysts and officers, police and other municipal departments, city agencies and elected officials, and all public safety practitioners and the public.

We have witnessed that in certain jurisdictions where the police have taken initiatives to contact residents about crime risk, the public has responded positively. We have documented how police agencies focused on risk management consider themselves as a resource to the community that is intended to reduce their vulnerability. Risk management is not something that police officers or analysts do in isolation. It is a central part of all police operations, with officers employing tools that give on-demand information to help them make better and more contextualized decisions. We have seen this in cities like Chicago and New York, with mobile data terminals and tablet computers that are utilized to push spatial intelligence to officers in the field. Actionable information and clever uses of communications technology allow police officers to make better situational decisions by anticipating how certain places might be vulnerable to crime.

Risk-based policing strategies informed by ACTION have led to new approaches to measuring police productivity that go beyond a heavy reliance on traditional law enforcement practices such as stops, arrests, or citations. Police have been able to measure their effects on mitigating the spatial influences of risky features—with the goal of reducing one or more risk factors' weights in postintervention RTMs, or, better yet, suppressing the risk factor's attractive qualities completely and removing it from the post model altogether. Imagine questions raised by commanders at a CompStat meeting about whether the relative risk values of targeted risk factors were lowered or removed from postintervention risk terrain models, and about the relationship these outcomes had on crime rates. This framework is apropos for the current demands on police departments by the constituents they serve—to demonstrate effectiveness without necessarily increasing arrest statistics (Sparrow, 2015).

Notifying others is heavily intertwined in public relations. In 2010, for instance, the police chief in Kansas City, Missouri, blogged about the department's use of RTM: how it encourages officers to think differently about solving crime problems, and how it changes the way limited resources are deployed for proactive engagement with the areas of highest risk. In 2013 the Fayetteville Police Department in North Carolina incorporated their risk-based intervention into the Community Wellness Plan, which was briefed by the police chief to the city council at the January meeting. In 2015, a press release for Atlantic City, New Jersey, resulted in the positive news headline "Places, Not People, Are the Focus of This New Crime-Fighting Data Analysis Tool" (Curry, 2015).

Our experiences collaborating with Kansas City, Fayetteville, Atlantic City, and other cities were instructive in terms of how to notify the community about risk reduction strategies and make police activities well known to the public they serve. ACTION should be a transparent, evidence-based approach to managing community risks in ways that are tailored to specific, real and perceived threats that upset people living there. ACTION can have a substantial positive effect on public safety through risk mitigation, and without a primary law enforcement focus on people, which could jeopardize community relations (Koss, 2015). Notifying others should be the people-oriented aspect of risk reduction strategies.

The complexities of risk management strategies may not fit into the day-to-day accounts of crime statistics. But the advantage of having clearly informed decisions that back up responses to (empirically documented) spatial risks goes a long way to provide context in which police officers, elected officials, the media, and the general public can judge the likelihood of successful outcomes and prospects for the problems faced in communities. Notifying others (via a variety of mediums) throughout the risk management process, including being honest about outcomes, facilitates these stakeholder relationships and increases the potential for long-term success.

NOTIFYING OTHERS

TIMING

During and after intervention activities are implemented. After outcome evaluations.

1. Frequent communication with key stakeholders.
2. Public relations.
3. Community awareness programs.
4. Transparency of policing practices, outcome measures, and evaluation results.

RISK REDUCTION

Looking at the interventions that have made use of risk terrain modeling in recent years, we have uncovered some interesting outcomes regarding the ways in which the police have used information about risky places. As depicted in figure 15, spatial intelligence is actualized in a variety of ways that fall within the range from simply "directing people where to go" to "directing multiple resources where to go, what to do when they get there, and why." Evidence suggests that both extremes have merit, depending on the intents and goals of the agency or its stakeholders.

The intervention planning intel report (IPIR) for Glendale, Arizona, suggested that robberies are likely intertwined with the actions of drug buyers in the city. People get robbed near ATMs on weekdays and near convenience stores (for their cell phones) on weekends. These two outlets for fast cash help fuel the purchase of drugs, which increases on the weekends. Risky places in Glendale were selected as target areas and, therefore, received more attention from the police, including high-visibility patrols, introductory and educational contacts with the public, and enhanced outreach and referrals to social services among drug users (buyers). The robbery rate in Glendale's target areas dropped significantly over three months; arrests did not increase in the target areas during the intervention. So, the police department's overall effectiveness increased not as a result of more arrests or related law enforcement actions, but as a result of their more focused and risk-based efforts within well-defined illegal behavior settings.

In other applications of RTM, risk terrain maps were used by police merely to determine where to go to find attractors and precipitators of illegal behavior. Comprehensive

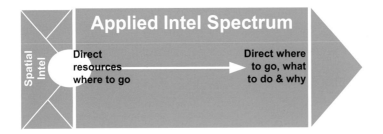

FIGURE 15
Spatial intelligence is actualized by police agencies in a variety of ways that fall within the range of options.

risk reduction strategies, however, should involve more than mobilizing only police; other agencies (for example, parole, probation, social service agencies, medical clinics, code enforcement, public works, sanitation, and so on) can monitor places over time to reduce the risks that such things as environment, poverty, recidivism, drug abuse, and so on might have on crime.

To expand risk reduction activities beyond police deployments or arrests, it is important to include data about communities that extend beyond crime incidents and into the contexts for crime that are formed by particular factors in the community. Allowing communities to suffer from decaying infrastructure, poor code enforcement, or inadequate sanitation can promote the types of problems that intensify risky places and support crime. Risk reduction strategies require fully informed risk narratives so that policies and practices can be proposed to mitigate spatial influences, modify deleterious conditions, bolster protective factors, and interrupt the interactions that lead to crime outcomes.

Currently popular policing strategies operate on the basis of responding to crime occurrence, targeting areas according to what has happened previously as a way of suggesting that if it happened in this location once, it will happen there again. An important aspect of risk reduction is that it extends beyond a focus on opportunities for crime and targets all aspects of the context that raises the risk that crime might occur. As we have emphasized throughout the book, spatial influence is a foundational concept for understanding and applying this framework. It suggests that we are able to extract from risk terrain models meaningful information for understanding criminal behavior patterns, for diagnosing attractors of existing crime clusters, and for forecasting places where new crimes are likely to emerge. So, it seems fitting to end this book with a conversation about the role of spatial influence in risk reduction.

THE COMMON THREAD OF SPATIAL INFLUENCE

As a principal approach to problem solving, risk reduction activities address the collective spatial influence of certain landscape features. The effect of spatial influence is not a constant but one that can be altered to reduce risk. So, spatial vulnerabilities are mitigated by focusing efforts on reducing or eliminating spatial influences, and not necessarily just the risky *features* themselves. If the spatial influences of risky features increase the chance of crime and its patterns over time, then it should be equally the case that reducing these spatial influences would reduce the incidence of crime. Risk reduction strategies based on spatial influence can involve a number of approaches that should be tailored to the specific study setting and informed by an IPIR and risk narrative.

We have spent a great deal of time studying the spatial influences of different qualities of space on crime outcomes. Most of these analyses have found that negative effects emerge from this influence (that is, "aggravating" risk terrain models). We can interpret this from two points of view. One is to consider how to reduce the negative spatial effects by dealing with their consequences, what we refer to as behavior settings that are problematic and conducive to crime. The treatment of these locations may be through interventions that impact human behaviors occurring there. The second viewpoint considers how we might moderate the negative affects of environmental features through a strategy that reinvests in locations to increase or enhance positive spatial influences of known protective features. This part of a risk reduction strategy focuses on how to not only remove the aggravating factors at risky places, but also replace them with protective factors, or detractors, of crime.

The Theory of Risky Places also reminds us that risky places are the product of both vulnerability and exposure, whereby the notion of spatial influence is woven throughout the concepts of risky features, vulnerable places, and local and global exposures to criminal events. The spatial influences of risky features in the environment contribute to attracting criminal behavior nearby; this is articulated using RTM. The spatial influence of instigator crimes attracts near repeats. Such local exposures to crime signal to motivated offenders that this place is good for (and thereby influences) the commission of new crimes. When many near repeat crimes occur at an area, hot spots form. Such global patterns of crime inform offender decision making and influence subsequent illegal behaviors, thereby perpetuating the hot spot. So, the rules that govern criminal behavior are executed on the basis of the spatial influences of risky features, instigator/near repeat crimes, and hot spots. These contributing factors of crime emergence and persistence can be moderated by addressing spatial influences—by focusing on risky features, by forthrightly managing deliberate and stochastic crime events at the most vulnerable places within a fixed period of time, and by preventing the clustering of crime incidents at the most vulnerable places over time.

Crime control is an inherently reactive endeavor for police. But risk management does not have to be. Focusing on spatial influences allows for a more proactive agenda. For instance, police may not have control over every situation in which crime events will occur (and crime is always probable, even in "low-crime" jurisdictions). But, among the crime events that are reported and known to police, task managers can control how resources are prioritized, allocated, and instructed to address specific incident locations based on known spatial vulnerabilities and recent past exposures. Because spatial influence is the measurable link between human behavior and place, it is also the most susceptible to intervention and reform. Managing risk, therefore, is reducing spatial influence.

REDUCING SPATIAL INFLUENCE: EXPOSURES

ACTION considers the role that changing situational factors might have on crime outcomes *and* provides a means to evaluate the overall effect of the risks presented by features that have strong influence in creating vulnerability and increased exposure to crime. This brings us back to case study number 1 in chapter 5, where we identified a three-part integration of RTM, hot spot mapping, and near repeat analysis for studying the spatial dynamics of crime. Let's expand on those ideas to propose tactical and strategic actions for risk reduction based on each method's information product, as exemplified in figure 16.[1] Few jurisdictions start with a clean slate and zero crime, so problems are often identified because crime incidents or hot spots already exist in an articulable way. In this scenario, the first step to study the spatial dynamics of crime (#1 in figure 16) is hot spot analysis to assess whether (and where) crimes cluster in the jurisdiction. The second step (#2 in figure 16) is risk terrain modeling to diagnose spatial factors of crime. The joint utility of information derived from steps 1 and 2 (A in figure 16) is to identify risky places in and around hot spot areas. The third step (#3 in figure 16) is near repeat analysis to assess the spatial-temporal patterns of crimes. The joint utility of information derived from steps 1 and 3 (B in figure 16) is a better understanding of spatial-temporal crime clusters. The joint utility of information derived from steps 2 and 3 (C in figure 16) is a nuanced understanding of risky places for initial and near repeat crimes.

The culmination of all three steps depicted in figure 16 results in information products that can inform short- and long-term strategic planning and at least three tactical deployment decisions. Information product A enables police to respond immediately to places where crimes cluster and crime problems persist, and to respond preemptively to vulnerable places. Information product B gives police temporal windows in which near repeat crimes are most likely to follow new crime events. This knowledge can help to reduce the costs of deploying extra resources for long or uncertain lengths of time following new crime incidents (Koper, 1995). This, in turn, can help to reduce alert fatigue among police officers assigned to patrol places near to new crime incidents (Johnson et al., 2007). Information product C allows police to prioritize place-based deployments of resources by comparing new crime incidents relative to all others according to the surrounding environment's suitability for hosting near repeat incidents. Priority can be given, and limited resources (re)allocated, to new crime incidents that have more high-risk "slices of the pie" than other incident locations. As illustrated in chapter 7, these techniques and information products are embodied within an IPIR. When considered

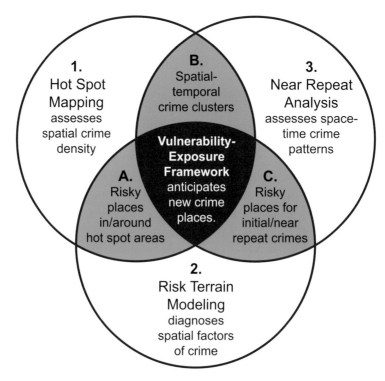

FIGURE 16

The vulnerability-exposure framework yields actionable information that can be used to anticipate new crime places. RTM adds environmental context to event-dependent hot spot and near repeat analyses.

jointly for ACTION, they broaden our approach to understanding the spatial dynamics of crime and overcome the limitations of strictly event-based inquiries and offender-centric responses.

REDUCING SPATIAL INFLUENCE: VULNERABILITY

Police responses to crime have traditionally been offender-focused and, thus, disconnected from the *spatial* analysis that informed the response. One benefit of risk terrain modeling that is especially apropos for a new era of policing is an emphasis on intervention activities that focus on places, not just people located at certain places. In a hour-long interview,[2] New York City Police Commissioner Bill Bratton explained how the latest manifestation of frayed relations between the police and Black communities was a byproduct of the implementation of CompStat in the 1990s. CompStat was developed as a means to communicate timely information about crime events and threats, and to identify emerging patterns and trends, based on administrative crime records. Sherman, Gartin, and Buerger's (1989) inaugural place-based research in Minneapolis,

Minnesota, brought hot spot mapping to the fore of evidence-based crime analysis and CompStat. This created new demand for police resources to be focused on high-crime (hot spot) areas. The treatment prescribed for hot spot areas in New York City was a Broken Windows style of policing, explained Bratton, where lower-level offenses were given higher priority and police officers were mandated to measure productivity and demonstrate success on the job by stopping, frisking, citing, and arresting individuals located in spatially defined problem areas. Ultimately, minority communities bore the brunt of this focused attention and treatment by police. Notably, such practices ordered by police commanders were not enjoyed by line-level officers, as they saw firsthand (and early on) the rift that policies of stop, question, and frisk (SQF) created between them and the public they served.

Bratton explained how police commanders forced these policies and practices at the behest of elected officials. And while political administrations changed over the years, police officers remained in the line of duty with the burden of these prescribed mandates, oftentimes against officers' better judgments. For decades, SQF was applied too extensively, Bratton said. But the cops were not the cause or the reason for this activity that created immense resentment toward the New York City Police Department (NYPD) by the minority communities, Bratton concluded. The cops bore the brunt of ill will from this crime problem "remedy" that was forced on them by multiple political administrations, he explained.

One lesson from this is that crime statistics alone should not dictate police action. Simmering frustrations and frayed relations between police and the public they serve can be exacerbated when crime analyses and intelligence products fail to elucidate root attractors of illegal behavior, especially when responses to spatial intelligence fail to acutely address the qualities of places and fail to look beyond merely the people located there. We have witnessed many disconnects between crime intelligence products, policies, and policing practices. One of these, as articulated by Bratton in New York City, occurs when a statistical assessment process focuses on crime counts and locations, and then when the response plan focuses almost exclusively on people at certain places (that is, it ignores the spatial attractors of illegal behavior located there). Second, disconnect often happens when measures of police productivity are reliant on the persistence of the illegal activities that are sought to be prevented (that is, such as when productivity measures depend on people being stopped, ticketed, or arrested), rather than on more sustainable and benign measures, such as efforts or actions associated with reducing spatial influences of risky features.

Sparrow (2015) wrote a provocative article about measuring performance in a modern police organization. He argues that reported crime rates will always be important indicators for police departments. However, substantial and recurrent reductions in crime figures are only possible when crime problems have first grown out of control. A sole reliance on the metric of crime reduction, Sparrow explained, would "utterly fail" to reflect the very best performance in crime control practices when police actions are successful at keeping crime rates low and stopping emerging crime problems before they grow (p. 5). Beyond looking at crime rate changes, a risk reduction approach to solving crime problems can suggest success in interventions when factors other than crime counts improve. So, risk reduction strategies have dual objectives: one to reduce crime counts and the other to reduce the spatial influences of known risk factors.

Another takeaway from New York City's history is that interventions by police or other stakeholders at hot spot areas should be robust, sustainable, and flexible. Crime events do not occur out of spatial context. Offenders may be aware of global patterns of crime, which inform their decision making and subsequent behaviors. But hot spots nevertheless emerge at the global level from the interactions that take place among individuals at the local level. Therefore, risk reduction strategies should deliberately focus on the offenders' behavior settings by mitigating the spatial influences of environmental features that attract, generate, or enable illegal behavior. Risk reduction actions that curb spatial vulnerability and the subsequent rate of crime events at places will lead the place to experience less crime and, thus, be less problematic in the long term. It may seem reasonable that targeting individual offenders at risky places would remove the chance of reoccurrence of crime and reduce its rate. But vulnerable environments need to be reformed to effectively control crime, or else new offenders will take the place of old. When law enforcement relies exclusively on deterrence and incapacitation in high-crime areas, it is rarely effective or equitable, particularly regarding minority neighborhoods (Braga & Weisburd, 2010).

In a meta-analysis that they performed on 11 intervention programs, Braga and Weisburd (2010) report that decreases in crime related not only to the offender-centric strategies but also to steps taken to modify the environments in which they operate. This finding and others presented throughout this book complement psychological research that reveals how treatments focused on people to change behaviors only work on behaviors that people do not do frequently. If people do the behavior enough in the same setting, the physical environment (itself) shapes the human behavior (even unconsciously). Psychologists refer to this as "outsourcing" control of behavior to the physical environment (Spiegel, 2015). When the environment consciously or unconsciously influences behavior, the only way to change human behavior for the long term is to alter the environment or the action sequences. Research suggests that this will have the best probability of changing outcomes (Louiselli & Cameron, 1998; Kennedy & Forde, 1998).

The social relevancy of risky features also affects their spatial influences at different times and under particular circumstances. This can make interactions among people and their geographies deeply fluid and something that must be considered with regard to risk reduction strategies. A spatiotemporal analysis of violent crime trauma hot spots in Vancouver, Canada, found several patterns of injury embedded in neighborhood characteristics, with nightclubs located in socioeconomically deprived neighborhoods the most prevalent risk factor (Walker, Schuurman, & Hameed, 2014). Researchers proposed "upstream" interventions to reduce the likelihood of violence, such as information posters placed in nightclub washrooms (a technique, they stated, that was used successfully in antismoking campaigns). They also proposed planning and modification of the built environment to prevent violence. For example, they understood crowded bars and crowded streets at closing times to be precipitators of interpersonal violence, and suggested modifications to widen sidewalks and improve nightclub design. Walker, Schuurman, and Hameed's (2014) study did not use RTM (to our knowledge), but as a risk-oriented research project, they further demonstrate how proactive remedies can be made to change environments *and* actors' action sequences before expected (undesirable) outcomes happen.

OUTCOME MEASURES

Risk reduction strategies to combat crime should result in a crime reduction. But another outcome measure of risk reduction activities that are informed by RTM should be mitigated spatial influences of one or more aggravating risk factors in the risk terrain model (or enhanced spatial influences of factors in a protective model). Interventions should aim to reduce crime counts by altering illegal behavior settings. Such impacts can be measured via comparisons of pre- and post-risk terrain models under the hypothesis that intervention activities will reduce the relative risk values for risk factors specifically and intentionally addressed by the intervention. Ideally, the intervention would render the targeted risk factors insignificant and, thus, exclude them from the postintervention risk terrain model altogether. Repeated iterations of this type of risk mitigation evaluation may be used to heuristically assess the changing qualities of places and associated spatial vulnerabilities throughout a study setting (with comparisons to control areas). This reduces the burden of reliance on traditional offender-centric law enforcement actions.

Police actions have an important role to play in affecting the risk terrain. They can deter offenders, embolden victims, and assist in the hardening of targets. These products can have the overall impact of reducing crime occurrence, but we need to separate what we would see as risk reduction strategies from prevention and response. A risk reduction strategy that follows ACTION requires that we identify the environmental conditions in which crime is likely to appear, according to diagnostics from risk terrain models. We then propose strategies to address these conditions and interrupt the interactions that lead to illegal behavior settings and crime outcomes. Police dealings with people at hot spots may have the effect of deterring criminals or even reducing crime counts at these areas in the short term. But, despite this, the underlying spatial factors that attract and generate problems in these areas do not go away. So, three things can happen: crime disappears, it displaces, or it subsides to reemerge later.

An important aspect of a risk reduction strategy is that while it can accommodate the ideas of situational crime prevention in targeting certain locations for intervention, the efforts extend beyond a focus on opportunities for crime or the "crime triangle," and instead target all aspects of the context that raises the risk that crime will occur. RTM provides an approach to understanding crime occurrence by identifying the relative influences of factors that contribute to it; risk terrain maps inform decisions about which places or areas can be targeted to reduce these risks. This is inherent in ACTION, which considers the effects of guardianship, victim characteristics, locations, precipitators, exposures, and offenders in a risk narrative that is contextually dynamic. Reiterations of RTM and reconsiderations of risk narratives make risk reduction activities transparent, measurable, and testable.

RTM AND PREDICTION

RTM is sometimes confused with event-based predictive analysis, but it is not the same. RTM is more advantageous to practitioners because successful responses to risky places can be measured, regardless of outcomes. Predictions about specific crime outcomes are deterministic in that an event is assumed to happen unless proper actions are taken; any occurrence of the predicted event connotes a failure of the police who were tasked with prevention, while any absence of the predicted event connotes either an adequate police response or a failed predictive model. Unfortunately, in this approach, the only true measure of success of a predictive model is for the event to occur, which is generally not in the publics' or practitioners' best interest. This is why most responses to predictive analyses are deemed failures when crime events occur—though the analytical technique itself may be applauded. Activities performed in response to predictions always have the burden of proving that those activities directly resulted in the nonevent—while assuming that the event would absolutely have occurred otherwise. While event-based predictive analytics focus on the presence or absence of an incident, RTM focuses on the dynamic settings where illegal behavior is most likely to result in crime occurrence. The unit of analysis is the place. So, the identification of vulnerable places permits police and other stakeholders to intervene and manage risk at the unit of analysis that they are operationally conditioned for—the geography. In this way, risk management and risk reduction activities performed by public safety practitioners can be appropriately credited with success and judged against the probable consequences of alternative or nonexistent engagements.

EPILOGUE

Giving high regard to spatial risks makes theoretical and intuitive sense: offenders know that they take risks and that these risks increase in certain locations; and police are deployed throughout spaces to combat crime and manage other real or perceived public safety and security threats. Utilizing environmental factors for crime diagnostics and forecasting has many benefits. One of these is that it enables intervention activities to focus on places, not just people located at certain places. Legal scholars (Ferguson, 2012; Koss, 2015) explain that RTM offers police an exceptional opportunity to quantify "high-crime" areas in a way that respects constitutional protections for citizens. This is because RTM enables a concerted effort to understand and address the mechanisms that enable crime hot spots to emerge and persist over time. RTM produces quantifiable outputs to inform policing strategies and, according to Koss (2015), generating such outputs for where to police can safeguard residents' Fourth Amendment rights.

Another benefit is that RTM is a sustainable technique because past crime data are not always needed to continue to make valid forecasts. Police throughout the world use RTM to be problem-oriented and proactive, to prevent new crimes without concern that a high success rate (and no new crime data) will hamper their ability to make new forecasts. Police are able to measure their effects on mitigating the spatial influences of risky features, and to judge their productivity without the burden of relying on crimes to occur and be reported. With RTM, police define their own intended foci and intents of policing actions, record productivity data accordingly, and then measure success by reevaluating one or more risk factors' weights in postintervention risk terrain models.

Ideally, their actions suppress a risk factor's attractive qualities completely, rendering it empirically absent from the post model altogether. Reported crime rate reductions will always be an important performance measure for police agencies. But RTM removes the need for a sole dependency on them.

A risky place is a particular portion of space that is influenced by the factors of spatial vulnerability and local and global information about crime events, particularly when they are considered together rather than in isolation. Such integration is justified by the Theory of Risky Places and is operationalized through analytical methods presented in an IPIR. Crime events emerge in a dynamic landscape of vulnerabilities and exposures that may be mediated through a constellation of factors beyond only those that are spatial. That is why strategic and tactical applications of RTM also require a consideration of event context. Event context helps to make the spatial intelligence more actionable and enables a refined development of risk-based decision making that can have profound implications for police practice and public safety. Spatial influence is the common thread for measuring and articulating the elements of risky places. As the measurable link between human behavior and risk factors at places, spatial influence is the most susceptible to intervention and reform, making it the common target of mitigation efforts. The key, then, is to focus efforts on reducing or eliminating spatial influences and not necessarily the risky *features* themselves.

Some people consider the data analysis using RTM as the starting and ending point in studying problems in their jurisdictions. Their RTM analyses are treated as statistical exercises to identify the most important factors in creating conditions for crime to occur. But this approach does little to consider the larger enterprise of risk management from the spatial risk perspective. Risk terrain modeling is one part of a larger risk management agenda that operationalizes and measures problems, suggests ways in which they can be addressed through interventions, proposes measures for assessing effectiveness of treatment and sustainability of efforts, and offers suggestions for how police organizations can be reconstituted as risk management agencies that address vulnerabilities and exposures in the communities that they serve through strategies that go beyond specific deterrence of offenders.

To exemplify, Jersey City, New Jersey, embraced risk-based policing as part of its Project Safe Neighborhoods (PSN) initiative.[1] At a 2015 task force meeting to discuss the IPIR for "aggravated violent crimes," a conversation was stimulated by "gas stations," one of the highest-risk factors identified by RTM. Gas stations had face validity to police officers in the room, as robberies, carjackings, and assaults were believed to be targeted at gas station attendants or unwary customers fueling their vehicles. A review of recent-past incident report narratives confirmed this event context in instances where "gas stations" were mentioned. But, furthermore, one stakeholder from a local agency who works with community youth suggested that not all gas station facilities should be treated as equal. She explained: Many unsupervised youth hang out after school around corner stores or bodegas, where they can easily congregate and get food, drinks, and rolling paper for smoking marijuana at nearby vacant buildings. This, she said, is what some kids in the neighborhood told her they do. But a city ordinance that requires bodegas to close at 10 PM (enacted in response to violence occurring around these facilities during nighttime hours) exempted gas stations with food marts. These gas stations, often open 24 hours, provide the space and supplies for youth to hang out late at night. This group of juveniles with some money to spend and little else to do, she explained, may create a unique context for turf conflict, offending, or victimization. Representatives from the Department of Public Works (DPW) added to the conversation with a proposal to prioritize DPW's HUD-style boarding-up of vacant buildings near to gas stations with food marts.[2] And the Mayor's Office and Department of Parks and Recreation proposed enhancing their advertising and recruitment campaigns for summer recreation activities and job opportunities at gas stations and places nearby. Police then agreed to deploy directed patrols and meet-and-greets with managers at these high-risk facilities at specific times of the day (based on their case file reviews and the newfound connections made between violent crime events and gas stations). Patrol officers will also make referrals to the in-house licensed social worker when juveniles in the area appear to be in need of outreach or support services. Officers also have an updated protocol for crime reporting citywide, where they are to inquire with victims and witnesses about possible connections of crime incidents to the known spatial risk factors (for example, Was the victim on the premise, coming from, or going to a *gas station* before the robbery?). They will then record identified connections in police reports so that risk narratives can be better articulated during the next iteration of ACTION.

IT'S ONLY SORT OF ALL ABOUT THE DATA

Incorporating such a holistic approach to crime analysis and problem solving necessitates "buy-in" from agency leadership. This commitment must be institutionalized in a manner to ensure that upper-level executives and those under their command incorporate risk reduction strategies into daily operations. It also requires in-house expertise to manage and analyze reliable and valid datasets. The efficient and effective use of RTM is dependent upon the availability and accessibility of data, as well as the intensity with which police commanders and other key stakeholders desire and attempt to understand it. As Joel Hunt, Senior Computer Scientist for the National Institute of Justice, says, it's not about "big data"; it's about "smart data." Using data smartly in policing necessitates the employ of information technologists to manage reliable and valid datasets so that decision makers and practitioners can "trust" the sources they rely on to execute thoughtful decisions and actions.

Data become more insightful with the fusion of crime analysts, information technologists, and police dispatchers who are capable of (and dedicated to) being the brokers of research-to-practice and practice-to-research. This synergy may materialize in the form of specific hires, consultants, or new training and continuing education to advance the skillsets of existing personnel. Regardless of the mechanism for acquiring such human capital, data managers and analysts should not be undervalued or overlooked in a risk management enterprise. Their value has further manifested in the United States with the development of real-time crime centers (Fox, 2014) that aim to manage multiple layers of data and translate all inputs into critical intelligence that can be communicated instantaneously to resources in the field.

Real-time information about risky features further exposes risk heterogeneity. For example, apartment buildings were a significant risk factor across all models for robberies in Glendale, Arizona. But apartment complexes experiencing a sharp increase in drug-related calls-for-service (that is, another risk factor) may be more criminogenic (at that period in time) than complexes where reported drug activity is stable. Police deployments and measures of outcome evaluations often begin and end in the custody of information and communications professionals, so these people and their tools should be factored into any risk management enterprise. Tools include investments in software, such as computerized record management systems (RMS) and GIS, and modern computer hardware that exceeds minimum requirements of software applications. We understand that police agencies generally have tight budgets, but there are many ways to keep costs low, including the use of very powerful, free, and open-sourced software. Cultural shifts within police agencies away from "crime fighting" and toward "risk management" cost very little financially. Coupled with sustainable investments in human capital, smart data, continuing education, and current technology, risk-based policing can go a long way to help agencies fight and prevent crime. Recent uses of RTM in various practical settings suggest that police departments are able to incorporate these investments into their agencies and utilize risk data within their analytical and cultural frameworks with measured success.

Key to the success of this paradigm is the willingness of police officers at all levels to ask new questions, collect new data, and find value in the results. It will be challenging for a police agency to routinely incorporate crime risk management into its operations if noncrime risk factor datasets, such as liquor licenses, business addresses, or noncriminal complaints, are collected unsystematically. Nonemergency services systems data, 3-1-1 government information, and other noncrime data, for instance, can be queried for complaints that point to locations of disorder, precipitators of crime, or other conditions that could support illegal behavior. If these data are collected ad hoc and mined to shed light on how disorder forms, then we could be even better able to anticipate where crime is likely to emerge. Chicago, Illinois, is one, but certainly not the only, illustration (see Caplan, Kennedy, Barnum, & Piza, 2015) of this with regard to RTM. Table 15 shows that 15 risk factors are spatially related to the 17,682 burglary incidents in Chicago in 2013. Proximity to foreclosed properties, abandoned vehicles, and burned-out alley lights were among the most important factors. Measures of two of these factors were obtained from 3-1-1 service request datasets. Once risk factors derived from noncrime data are identified, stakeholders can explore the

TABLE 15   Risk Factors for Burglary in Chicago

Risk Factor	Count	Coefficient	Spatial Operationalization	Spatial Influence (ft)	RRV
3-1-1 Service Requests for Street Lights Out	9,999	0.1595	Proximity	852	1.1730
3-1-1 Service Requests for Alley Lights Out	9,995	0.4605	Proximity	852	1.5848
3-1-1 Service Requests for Abandoned Vehicles	7,137	0.6955	Proximity	1,704	2.0046
Apartment Complexes	391	0.1434	Proximity	3,408	1.1542
Foreclosures	15,305	1.3849	Proximity	852	3.9944
Problem Buildings	28,575	0.6645	Density	852	1.9434
Gas Stations	140	0.1747	Proximity	3,408	1.1909
Grocery Stores	933	0.2477	Proximity	1,704	1.2810
Laundromats	173	0.1202	Density	3,408	1.1278
Retail Shops	235	0.1016	Density	3,408	1.1070
Schools	1,021	0.3264	Proximity	1,704	1.3860
Variety Stores	124	0.1397	Density	3,408	1.1499
Bars	1,316	0.2013	Density	3,408	1.2230
Nightclubs	128	0.1946	Density	1,704	1.2148
Bus Stops	10,711	0.2525	Proximity	1,704	1.2873
Intercept	–	–4.1782	–	–	–

Banks	367				
Health Care Centers and Gyms	176				
Homeless Shelters	29				
Malls	29				
Parking Stations and Garages	218				
Post Offices	53				
Recreation Centers	33				
Rental Halls	89				
Liquor Stores	926				

(likely) mechanisms through which risks are presented and then initiate risk reduction activities. In Chicago, the police department developed strategies to work with other city officials, including the Housing Authority, to target foreclosed and other problem buildings using city ordinance enforcement to improve conditions conducive to crime. They also worked with private lenders to address the broader scope of the foreclosure crisis.

Kinney et al. (2008) suggest that environments may also include crime detractors, that is, characteristics that push people away and contain few attractions for crime. This points to the fact that places can be dynamic, and that protective features may also be considered in a risk narrative. The concept of crime detractors implies recognition among people who frequent certain places that things can be done to reduce the negative qualities. In lower-risk settings, risk reduction strategies should be directed at enhancing the strength and scope of detractors and managing places with the aim that they do not become vulnerable for illegal behavior and susceptible to the long-term consequences of repeat crimes or hot spots. This requires special consideration of the fact that the legitimate and legal behaviors happening in these areas may provide some rationale behind the colocation of criminal activities. So, reducing the likelihood of criminal behaviors at lower-risk settings requires an understanding of this codependence and the implications that exist in restricting one set of behaviors while not canceling legitimate ones.

As we wrap up this book, let's reinforce the fact that RTM is very doable. It only requires people to think spatially and act rationally. We have covered a lot of material and shared many insights about RTM and risk management throughout these chapters. It may feel a bit overwhelming. But the key to utilizing RTM successfully is to start using it. Start on a small scale, with an acute problem, or with "practice" data. Prepare intervention planning intel reports (IPIRs) with crime analysis methods that you are already comfortable with, to try integrating insights from results across multiple methods in a way that informs a risk narrative; *then* add RTM for further explication. Involve a few peers in ACTION tabletop exercises to discuss draft templates of IPIRs formatted to be most appropriate for your agency, jurisdiction, and objectives; and design risk reduction strategies in a manner that would not place an undue burden on agency resources or finances. That is, the risk reduction activities should be considered reasonably sustainable and repeatable under normal (for example, non-grant-funded) conditions. This is especially important when the strategies prove effective because it allows them to continue.

This book begins to fill the void of evidence-based spatial intelligence that public safety practitioners can use to assess and manage risks of crime at places throughout their jurisdictions. Even if crimes do not cluster spatially in a jurisdiction, there can be meaningful and statistically significant spatial correlates of incident locations that can be used to assess future risks. RTM is being used by researchers, policy makers, and practitioners to help explain *why* spatial patterns of crime exist in a jurisdiction, and *what can be done* to mitigate risky places. Certain features of the environment will create behavior settings with exceptionally strong likelihoods for criminal events. RTM articulates these vulnerable places and advances our understanding of the spatial dynamics of crime.

GLOSSARY

ACTION (ACRONYM) A pragmatic focus on Assessment, Connections, Tasks, Interventions, Outcomes, and Notifications that is applied consistently across projects and study settings.

AREA A part of space defined as two or more contingent places.

ATTRACTORS (OF CRIME) Features of the environment that entice offenders to places to commit crime.

CRIME An act of commission or omission that constitutes prosecution by the state and is punishable by law.

EMERGENCE The process of a place coming into being as important or prominent, for example, with the frequent occurrence of crime incidents; relates to the extent and concentration of spatial influences, where spatial context of the landscape is likely to increase potential for new crime incidents.

EVENT CONTEXT A situational-based understanding of crime incidents that looks at behavioral outcomes as less deterministic and more a function of a dynamic interaction among people that occurs at places.

EXPOSURE The historical facts and collective memories people have about places and the events that occurred there; existing knowledge of offenders and crime hot spots.

GENERATORS (OF CRIME) Represented by increased opportunities for crime that emerge from the collection of more people into areas following specific types of behavior, simply because of the increased volume of interaction taking place in these areas.

GEOGRAPHIC INFORMATION SYSTEM (GIS) A computer software application for managing, editing, analyzing, and displaying data that are spatially referenced to the Earth; a tool that supports the dimension of spatial analysis for research and evaluation by providing an interface between data and a map.

INTELLIGENCE, INTEL Acquired or applied knowledge; secret, confidential, or proprietary information for decision making; information for tactical or strategic operations. See also Spatial Intelligence.

MODELING Attributing the presence, absence, influence, or intensity of qualities of the real world to places within a terrain, to study their simultaneous effect on the risk for undesired outcomes.

PLACE A particular portion of space where activities or functions may occur; the micro unit of analysis for risk terrain modeling.

RISK A consideration of the probabilities of particular outcomes; the probability of an occurrence of an undesired outcome (for example, crime) determined by the increased spatial vulnerability at places.

RISK MANAGEMENT An information gathering and analysis process, focused on a particular problem or set of problems, which integrates multiple methods and allows insights from each to prescribe ways in which to address problems or minimize their impact. ACTION is a component of risk management that produces spatial intelligence.

RISK NARRATIVE A spoken or written account of connected events. It is a story, so to speak, about how events, such as crimes, relate to other phenomena in their environments.

RISK TERRAIN MODELING A risk assessment technique and diagnostic method for identifying the spatial attractors of criminal behavior and environmental factors that are conducive to crime.

RISKY PLACE A particular portion of space that has been assessed for its likelihood of experiencing a particular outcome and to which a value has been attributed, thereby allowing for relative comparisons among places throughout a landscape; formed as a result of the confluence of the spatial influences of certain factors combined with conditions of exposure derived from past crime events; result from an overall assessment of vulnerability and exposures throughout the landscape.

RTMDX UTILITY Software application that automates risk terrain modeling.

SOCIAL RELEVANCY Pertinence to society; practical and social applicability to human behavior and peoples' uses of space at certain times and settings; a concept to recognize that interactions among people and their geographies are deeply fluid, in that no landscape feature retains its spatial influence and applicability to human behavior permanently.

SPACE A continuous expanse within which things exist and move.

SPATIAL INFERENCE Regards interactions that occur among features to support criminal behavior; a concept to suggest that one is able to extract from a risk terrain model meaningful information for understanding criminal behavior patterns, for diagnosing attractors of existing crime clusters, and for forecasting places where new crimes are likely to emerge.

SPATIAL INFLUENCE The way in which features of an environment affect behaviors at or around the features themselves; the measurable link between features of a landscape and their impacts on people and the ways in which they use space; the articulation of perceptual cues observed about features and gleaned from personal opinions, experiences, and empirical knowledge about similar features or characteristics thereof under other similar circumstances.

SPATIAL INTELLIGENCE The communication and application of spatial inferences for deliberate action.

SPATIAL RISK PERSPECTIVE Approach to (crime) analysis that suggests a way of looking at behavioral outcomes as less deterministic and more a function of a dynamic interaction among people that occurs at places.

STRATEGIC The identification of long-term agency-wide aims and interests, and carefully designed means of achieving them, for a particular purpose.

TACTICAL Carefully tailored actions for use in immediate support of policing operations, given the known facts and conditions relevant to an event; thoughtful responses and purposeful small-scale actions with an immediate end in view.

TERRAIN A study extent of equally sized places (for example, raster cells) whose attributes quantify vulnerabilities at each place.

THEORY OF RISKY PLACES Proposes that risk levels of crime can be computed at places according to the symbiotic effects of three sets of factors (spatial vulnerability, global exposure, and local exposure); looks at patterns, rhythms, and tempos of criminal behavior within a vulnerability-exposure framework that computes the relationship between context, process, and threat.

TRANSLATIONAL CRIMINOLOGY The process of taking research and putting it into practice.

VULNERABILITY (SPATIAL) The context of environmental risk; a place's vulnerability is operationalized by the spatial influences of nearby features.

NOTES

CHAPTER 2. RISK TERRAIN MODELING METHODS

1. The educational version of the RTMDx Utility is free for noncommercial use. The professional version of the Utility is bundled with the RTM Training Webinar, offered regularly by the Rutgers Center on Public Security.
2. NIJ Award No. 2012-IJ-CX-0038.
3. This was done using the RTMDx Polygon-to-Points Tool for ArcGIS, which is available for free at rutgerscps.org.
4. Some early RTM studies tested risk terrain models for gun shootings with logistic regression (Caplan, Kennedy, & Miller, 2011; Kennedy et al., 2011). In logistic regression, the dependent variable (that is, gun shootings) is dichotomized to represent either the presence ("1") or absence ("0") of one or more incidents. In the case of shootings, logistic regression tests the influence of the independent variable(s) (for example, "risk values") on the presence or absence of any shooting incidents. Given the infrequent occurrence of shootings (compared to other crime types), and the fact that most spatial units (that is, cells) are unlikely to have more than one incident, logistic regression can be an appropriate statistical test in such cases. However, for more frequently occurring crime types, logistic regression may undercount the total number of crimes since multiple incidents are collapsed into a single cell to fulfill the requirements of logistic regression. Such undercounting of incidents may depreciate the validity of the model, particularly by underestimating the predictive capacity of risk terrain models (Piza, 2012).

5. Results from a Poisson goodness-of-fit test confirmed that the 2013 robbery incident locations (the dependent variable) would best be modeled with a negative binomial regression (Pearson gof = 63810.22, p<0.001).

CHAPTER 3. CRIME EMERGENCE, PERSISTENCE, AND EXPOSURE

1. See also Irvin-Erickson, 2015: www.ncjrs.gov/pdffiles1/nij/grants/248636.pdf.
2. Defined as "the taking or attempting to take anything from the care, custody, or control of a person or persons by force or threat of force or violence and/or by putting the victim in fear."

CHAPTER 5. THE THEORY OF RISKY PLACES

1. Caplan, Kennedy, & Piza, 2013a.
2. The complete results of this study can be viewed at Caplan et al., 2013.
3. A raster grid in a GIS was used to model places throughout the Irvington landscape. Cells of 100 feet by 100 feet comprised the grid and served as the standard unit of analysis. This allowed us to model risky places as precisely as one corner or the middle of a street block, and was considered to be the smallest spatial unit to which police could reasonably be deployed.
4. The NN index is expressed as the ratio of the observed distance divided by the expected distance, that is, the average distance between neighbors in a hypothetical random distribution. If the index is less than 1, the pattern exhibits clustering; if the index is greater than 1, the trend is toward dispersion.
5. Pearson Chi-Squared value = 2.78; df = 1; p<0.10.
6. It uses the XY-coordinate and date of criminal incidents to test for statistically significant spatial-temporal patterns between all points within the dataset. The patterns found are then compared to an expected pattern if no near repeat phenomenon exists using the Monte Carlo method.
7. Iterations requested: 99, Spatial bands/bandwidth: 10/100, Temporal bands/bandwidth: 24/7; Manhattan.
8. Iterations requested: 99, Spatial bands/bandwidth: 10/100, Temporal bands/bandwidth: 24/7; Manhattan.
9. Iterations requested: 999, Spatial bands/bandwidth: 10/100, Temporal bands/bandwidth: 12/14; Manhattan.
10. For a detailed explanation of the data sources and operationalizations of the risk factor datasets, see Caplan et al., 2013a.
11. Moran's Index = -0.001583; Expected Index = -0.000248; Variance = 0.000197; Z Score = -0.095161; p-value = 0.924187.
12. Conceptually, risk is rarely or never absolutely zero. Therefore, environmental risk values of zero should be interpreted as the risk for crime at these places being no greater than any other place under normal circumstances.
13. Pearson Chi-Square = 31.40, p<0.001, n = 4039.

14. -2 Log Likelihood = 335.789; Nagelkerke R Square = 0.025; B = 2.365; S.E. = 0.629; Wald = 14.15; df = 1; p<0.001; Exp[B] = 10.645; 95% C.I. = 3.104–36.502.

15. The layers were not mutually exclusive. However, spatial influence of the convenience store gas stations may be different from the overall dataset, so it made sense to test them on their own.

16. Done using the "other functions" tool in the near repeat calculator, determining which incidents in a near repeat pair were the instigator and near repeat incidents.

CHAPTER 6. EVENT CONTEXTS OF RISKY PLACES

1. See also Caplan, Marotta, Piza, & Kennedy, 2014.

2. According to CPD officials, "assault" is defined as threats of bodily harm, and can cover a broad range of incidents against police, from resisting arrest without any injury to the police officer to threatening the officer with a weapon (but not using it). "Battery" is the intentional causing of serious bodily harm or the attempt to cause serious bodily harm or death. Battery, by legal definition, requires physical contact, which is more likely to result in felonious injury or death to police in the line of duty. Battery also has a narrower scope than assault and is a bit more distinct for operational purposes. The personal risk to police officers from battery is also greater than from assault in that some degree of physical injury is likely an outcome.

3. Some jurisdictions use the terms "battery" or "assault" interchangeably. Others define "assault" as the threat of bodily harm and "battery" as physical contact resulting in harm, serious bodily injury, or death. Much of the literature reviewed here uses these concepts interchangeably to imply any form of violence toward law enforcement, including physical contact. All battery/assault toward law enforcement is considered "felonious," meaning that they were intentional, aggravated, and illegal in nature as opposed to accidental (for example, such as harm caused by a trip and fall).

4. Buildings become "problem buildings" when a report is received via a 3-1-1 complaint from a citizen or from the police or other city official in regards to the specific location. Reasons for such a report can be due to vacancy, drugs, gangs, and so on.

5. All batteries/assaults in 2012 were selected for this portion of the case study because it is inclusive of all the other categories of battery/assault to police officers that were tested earlier, and it offers the largest sample size to permit partitioning the data biannually and still retain sufficient power for regression modeling. That was the statistical justification. For practical purposes, police decision making and risk assessments to inform policies and protocols for responding to calls-for-service in certain places in the jurisdiction are informed by the broad category of recent-past events that could put officers at risk of personal injury or fatality. Here, that is "all batteries/assaults" because injury or fatality is predicated on the initial battery/assault of any degree of severity. Minor aggression can turn very serious very quickly. So, any and all battery/assault incidents matter.

6. Results from a Poisson goodness-of-fit test confirmed that the Period 2 battery/assault incident locations (the dependent variable) follow a Poisson distribution (Pearson gof = 34764.07, p<0.001).

7. Results from a Poisson goodness-of-fit test confirmed that the Period 2 battery/assault incident locations (the dependent variable) follow a negative binomial distribution (Pearson gof = 399.58, p<0.001).

8. It was also a manageable number of cases to qualitatively review for content (n = 26).

9. It is concerned with the effects of the natural and built environment on human behavior.

CHAPTER 7. RISK MANAGEMENT AND RTM IN ACTION

1. Here, based simply on twice the average NN distance of crimes in the jurisdiction.

2. The Glendale study referenced here used street segments as the unit of analysis, with variable values assigned as attributes for outcome evaluation tests. "Places," therefore, refer to "street segments" in this instance.

3. The intervention should be designed in a manner that does not place an undue burden on police department resources or finances. This means that the intervention's activities should be considered to be reasonably sustainable or repeatable under "normal conditions." If the interventions will be time-limited, consider the requirements for valid and reliable statistical impact assessments (that is, power).

4. For example, in Jersey City, New Jersey, we utilized temporal heat maps to consider focusing intervention activities at particular places only at certain times of the day. We also produced risk terrain models for particular police shifts (that is, three risk terrain models for each eight-hour shift), so consideration could be given to developing tailored intervention strategies for each shift. That is, some factors, such as schools or bars, may pose high risks during one time of the day but not during others—allowing for customized intervention strategies based on working shifts.

CHAPTER 8. RISK REDUCTION

1. This figure was adapted from Caplan, Kennedy, & Piza, 2013a.

2. On *Charlie Rose,* aired January 12, 2015, www.hulu.com/watch/737448.

EPILOGUE

1. http://grants.ojp.usdoj.gov:85/selector/awardDetail?awardNumber = 2014-GP-BX-0015&fiscalYear = 2014&applicationNumber = 2014-H2748-NJ-GP&programOffice = BJA&po = BJA.

2. HUD: US Department of Housing and Urban Development.

REFERENCES

Acharya, A. (2014). Big data for social good: 5 ways to a higher purpose. Retrieved from http://www.forbes.com/sites/netapp/2014/10/15/big-data-social-good/.

Alexiou, A. S. (2006). The death and life of great American cities. In *Jane Jacobs: Urban visionary* (pp. 68–94). New Brunswick, NJ: Rutgers University Press.

Andresen, M. (2014). Environmental criminology: Evolution, theory and practice. London: Routledge.

Andresen, M. A., & Malleson, N. (2011). Testing the stability of crime patterns: implications for theory and policy. *Journal of Research in Crime and Delinquency, 48*(1), 58–82.

Anselin, L., Cohen, J., Cook, D., Gorr, W., & Tita, G. (2000). Spatial analyses of crime. In D. Duffee (Ed.), *Measurement and analysis of crime and justice: Criminal justice 2000, vol. 4* (pp. 213–262). Washington, DC: US Department of Justice, National Institute of Justice.

Arlot, S. & Celisse, A. (2010). A survey of cross-validation procedures for model selection. *Statistics Surveys, 4,* 40–79.

Basta, L. A., Richmond, T. S., & Wiebe, D. J. (2010). Neighborhoods, daily activities, and measuring health risks experienced in urban environments. *Social Science and Medicine, 71*(11), 1943–1950.

Baum, A., Singer, J. E., & Baum, C. S. (1981). Stress and the environment. *Journal of Social Issues, 37,* 4–35.

Berkowitz, L. (1983). The experience of anger as a parallel process in the display of impulsive, "angry" aggression. In R. G. Green and E. I. Donnerstein (Eds.), *Aggression: Theoretical and empirical reviews, vol. 1* (pp. 103–133). New York, NY: Academic Press.

Block, R. L., & Block, C. R. (1995). Space, place, and crime: Hotspot areas and hot places of liquor related crime. In J. E. Eck & D. Weisburd (Eds.), *Crime and place, vol.* 4 (pp. 145–184). Monsey, NY: Criminal Justice Press.

Bohrer, S., Davis, E., & Garrity, T. (2000). Establishing a foot pursuit policy: Running into danger. *FBI Law Enforcement Bulletin*, 69(5), 10–15.

Bowers, K. J., & Johnson, S. D. (2005). Domestic burglary repeats and space-time clusters: The dimensions of risk. *European Journal of Criminology*, 2(1), 67–92.

Braga, A. A. (2004). Gun violence among serious young offenders. In *Problem-oriented guides for police: Problem-specific guides series.* Washington, DC: US Department of Justice, Office of Community Oriented Policing Services.

Braga, A. A. (2005). Hot spots policing and crime prevention: A systematic review of randomized controlled trials. *Journal of Experimental Criminology*, 1(3), 317–342.

Braga, A., & Bond, B. (2008). Policing crime and disorder hot spots: A randomized controlled trial. *Criminology*, 46(3), 577–607.

Braga, A., & Clarke, R. V. (2014). Explaining high-risk concentrations of crime in the city: Social disorganization, crime opportunities, and important next steps. *Journal of Research in Crime and Delinquency*, 51(4), 480–498.

Braga, A. A., Papachristos, A. V., & Hureau, D. M. (2012). The effects of hot spots policing on crime: An updated systematic review and meta-analysis. *Justice Quarterly*, 31(4), 633–663.

Braga, A. A., & Weisburd, D. (2010). *Policing problem places: Crime hot spots and effective prevention.* Oxford: Oxford University Press.

Braga, A. A., & Weisburd, D. L. (2012). The effects of focused deterrence strategies on crime: A systematic review and meta-analysis of the empirical evidence. *Journal of Research in Crime and Delinquency*, 49(3), 323–358.

Brandl, S. G., & Stroshine, M. S. (2003). Toward an understanding of the physical hazards of police work. *Police Quarterly*, 6(2), 172–191.

Brandl, S. G., & Stroshine, M. S. (2012). The physical hazards of police work revisited. *Police Quarterly*, 15(3), 262–282.

Brantingham, P., & Brantingham, P. (1981). *Environmental criminology.* Beverly Hills, CA: Sage.

Brantingham, P., & Brantingham, P. (1993). Nodes, paths, and edges: Considerations on the complexity of crime and the physical environment. *Journal of Environmental Psychology* 13, 3–28.

Brantingham, P., & Brantingham, P. L. (1995). Criminality of place: Crime generators and crime attractors. *European Journal on Criminal Policy and Research* 3, 1–26.

Burgess, E. W. (1928). Factors determining success or failure on parole. In A. A. Bruce, E. W. Burgess, & A. J. Harno (Eds.), *The workings of the indeterminate sentence law and the parole system in Illinois* (pp. 221–234). Springfield, IL: Illinois State Board of Parole.

Bursik, R. (1988). Social disorganization and theories of crime and delinquency: Problems and prospects. *Criminology*, 26(4), 519–551.

California Commission on Peace Officer Safety Training (POST). (2001). A five year study of law enforcement officers killed and assaulted in the line of duty: A 1995–1999 report. Sacramento, CA: POST Media Distribution Center. Retrieved from http://lib.post.ca.gov /Publications/55677885.pdf.

Caplan, J. M. (2003). Police cynicism: Police survival tool? *Police Journal, 76*(4), 304–313.

Caplan, J. M. (2011). Mapping the spatial influence of crime correlates: A comparison of operationalization schemes and implications for crime analysis and criminal justice practice. *Cityscape,* 13(3), 57–83.

Caplan, J. M., & Kennedy, L. W. (2010). *Risk terrain modeling manual: Theoretical framework and technical steps of spatial risk assessment.* Newark, NJ: Rutgers Center on Public Security.

Caplan, J. M. & Kennedy, L. W. (2013). *Risk terrain modeling diagnostics utility (version 1.0).* Newark, NJ: Rutgers Center on Public Security.

Caplan, J. M., Kennedy, L. W., Barnum, J. D., & Piza, E. L. (2015). Risk terrain modeling for spatial risk assessment. *Cityscape: A Journal of Policy Development and Research,* 17(1), 7–16.

Caplan, J. M., Kennedy, L. W., & Baughman, J. (2012). Kansas City's violent crime initiative. *Crime Mapping,* 4(2), 9–37.

Caplan, J. M., Kennedy, L. W., & Miller, J. (2011). Risk terrain modeling: Brokering criminological theory and GIS methods for crime forecasting. *Justice Quarterly,* 28(2), 360–381.

Caplan, J. M., Kennedy, L. W., & Piza, E. (2013a). Joint utility of event-dependent and environmental crime analysis techniques for violent crime forecasting. *Crime and Delinquency,* 59(2), 243–270.

Caplan, J. M., Kennedy, L. W., & Piza, E. (2013b). *Risk terrain modeling diagnostic user manual (version 1.0).* Newark, NJ: Rutgers Center on Public Security.

Caplan, J. M., Marotta, P., Piza, E. L., & Kennedy, L. W. (2014). Spatial risk factors of felonious battery to police officers. *Policing: An International Journal of Police Strategies & Management,* 37(4), 823–838.

Caplan, J. M., Piza, E. L., & Kennedy, L. W. (2012). Establishing situational context in risk terrains (Research brief). Newark, NJ: Rutgers Center on Public Security. Retrieved from http://rutgerscps.weebly.com/uploads/2/7/3/7/27370595/conjunctiveanalysis_insightsbrief.pdf.

Chainey, S., Tompson, L. & Uhlig, S. (2008). The utility of hotspot mapping for predicting spatial patterns of crime. *Security Journal,* 21, 4–28.

Chicago Police Department. (2010). Annual report. Retrieved from https://portal.chicago police.org/portal/page/portal/ClearPath/News/Statistical%20Reports/Annual%20 Reports/10AR.pdf.

Clarke, R. (1997). Introduction. In R. Clarke (Ed.), *Situational crime prevention, successful case studies* (2nd ed.). Monsey, NY: Criminal Justice Press.

Clarke, R., & Eck, J. (2005). *Crime analysis for problem solvers in 60 small steps.* Washington, DC: US Department of Justice Office of Community Oriented Policing Services.

Cohen, L. E., & Felson, M. (1979). Social change and crime rate trends: A routine activity approach. *American Sociological Review,* 44, 588–608.

Cohen, L., Kluegel, J., & Land, K. (1981). Social inequality and predatory criminal victimization: An exposition and test of a formal theory. *American Sociological Review,* 46(5), 505–524.

Compton, M. T., Bakeman, R., Broussard, B., Hankerson-Dyson, D., Husbands, L., Krishan, S., . . . & Watson, A. C. (2014). The police-based crisis intervention team (CIT) model: II. Effects on level of force and resolution, referral, and arrest. *Psychiatric Services.*

Compton, M. T., Neubert, B. N. D., Broussard, B., McGriff, J. A., Morgan, R., & Oliva, J. R. (2009). Use of force preferences and perceived effectiveness of actions among Crisis Intervention Team (CIT) police officers and non-CIT officers in an escalating psychiatric crisis involving a subject with schizophrenia. *Schizophrenia bulletin,* sbp146.

Cordner, G. (2006). People with mental illness. Washington, DC: United States Department of Justice, Office of Community Oriented Policing Services. Retrieved from http://cops.usdoj.gov/Publications/e04062003.pdf.

Cornish, D. B., & Clarke, R. V. (Eds.). (1986). *The reasoning criminal: Rational choice perspectives on offending.* New York, NY: Springer-Verlag.

Corso, A., Leroy, G., & Alsusdais, A. (2015). Toward predictive crime analysis via social media, big data, and GIS. iConference 2015. Retrieved from https://www.ideals.illinois.edu/bitstream/handle/2142/73457/229_ready.pdf?sequence = 2.

Couclelis, H. (1992). People manipulate objects (but cultivate fields): Beyond the raster-vector debate in GIS. In A. Frank, I. Campari, & U. Formentini (Eds.), *Theories and methods of spatio-temporal reasoning in geographic space* (pp. 65–77). New York, NY: Springer.

Covington, M. W., Huff-Corzine, L., & Corzine, J. (2014). Battered police: Risk factors for violence against law enforcement officers. *Violence and Victims,* 1(29), 34–52.

Curry, C. (2015). Places, not people, are the focus of this new crime-fighting data analysis tool. *Vice News,* October 15. Retrieved from https://news.vice.com/article/places-not-people-are-the-focus-of-this-new-crime-fighting-data-analysis-tool.

Detroit Police Department. (2010). Foot pursuit protocol. Retrieved from https://www.detroitmi.gov/Portals/0/docs/police/DPD%20Civil%20Rights/202.7%20Foot%20Pursuit.pdf.

Douglas, M. (1992). *Risk and blame: Essays in cultural theory.* London: Routledge.

Downs R. & Stea D. (1973). Cognitive maps and spatial behavior: Process and products. In R. Downs & D. Stea (Eds.), *Image and environment: Cognitive mapping and spatial behavior* (pp. 8–26). Chicago, IL: Aldine.

Drawve, G. (2014). A metric comparison of predictive hot spot techniques and RTM. *Justice Quarterly.* Advance online publication. doi:10.1080/07418825.2014.904393.

Drawve, G., Moak, S. C., & Berthelot, E. R. (2014). Predictability of gun crimes: A comparison of hot spot and risk terrain modelling techniques. *Policing and Society.* Advance online publication. doi:10.1080/10439463.2014.942851.

Dugato, M. (2013). Assessing the validity of risk terrain modeling in a European city: Preventing robberies in the city of Milan. *Crime Mapping: A Journal of Research and Practice,* 5(1), 63–89.

Eck, J. E. (1994). Drug markets and drug places: A case-control study of the spatial structure of illicit drug dealing (Unpublished doctoral dissertation). University of Maryland, College Park.

Eck, J. E. (2001). Policing and crime event concentration. In R. F. Meier, L. W. Kennedy, & V. F. Sacco (Eds.), *The process and structure of crime: Criminal events and crime analysis* (pp. 249–276). New Brunswick, NJ: Transactions.

Eck, J. E. (2002). Preventing crime at places. In L. W. Sherman, D. P. Farrington, B. C. Welsh, & D. L. MacKenzie (Eds.), *Evidence-based crime prevention* (pp. 241–294). New York, NY: Routledge.

Eck, J. E., Chainey, S., Cameron, J. G., Leitner, M., & Wilson, R. (2005). Mapping crime: Understanding hot spots. Washington, DC: National Institute of Justice.

Eck, J., Clarke, R., & Guerette, R. (2007). Ricky facilities: Crime concentration in homogeneous sets of establishments and facilities. *Crime Prevention Studies, 21,* 225–264.

Edmonds, W. & Mallard, J. (2011). *Using risk terrain modeling to analyze holiday robberies in Arlington, TX.* Paper presented at the training conference of the International Association of Crime Analysts, Hyannis, MA.

Edwards, T. D. (1995). Felonious killings of state police and highway patrol officers: A descriptive and comparative evaluation. *American Journal of Police, 14*(2), 89–105.

Egenhofer, M., & Mark, D. (1995). Naïve geography. In A. U. Frank & W. Kuhn (Eds.), *Spatial information theory—a theoretical basis for GIS, international conference COSIT '95, Semmering, Austria: Lecture Notes in Computer Science 988* (pp. 1–15). New York, NY: Springer-Verlag.

Ekblom, P. (1999). Can we make crime prevention adaptive by learning from other evolutionary struggles? *Studies of Crime and Crime Prevention, 8*(1), 27–51.

Ellis, D., Choi, A., & Blaus, C. (1993). Injuries to police officers attending domestic disturbances: An empirical study. *Canadian Journal of Criminology, 35,* 149.

Farrell, G., Phillips, C., & Pease, K. (1995) Like taking candy: Why does repeat victimization occur? *British Journal of Criminology, 35*(3), 384–399.

FBI. (2007). *Crime in the United States, 2007.* Retrieved from https://www2.fbi.gov/ucr/cius2007/offenses/violent_crime/murder_homicide.html.

FBI. (2012). Law enforcement officers killed and assaulted. Washington, DC: United States Department of Justice. Retrieved from http://www.fbi.gov/about-us/cjis/ucr/leoka/2011/about-law-enforcement-officers-killed-and-assaulted.

Felson, M. (1995). *Crime and nature.* Thousand Oaks, CA: Sage.

Ferguson, A. G. (2012). Predictive policing and reasonable suspicion. *Emory Law Review, 62,* 259–325.

Fisher, B., & Nasar, J. L. (1995). Fear spots in relation to microlevel physical cues: Exploring the overlooked. *Journal of Research in Crime and Delinquency, 32*(2), 214–239.

Ford, C. T. (2000). *Violence against police: Felonious killings of South Carolina police officers from 1962 to 1998 and assaults against South Carolina police officers in 1991 and 1997.* Ohio: Air Force Institute of Technology, Wright-Patterson Air Force Base.

Fox, M. (2014). How real time crime center technologies are force multipliers. Retrieved from http://www.policeone.com/police-products/police-technology/articles/7083433-How-real-time-crime-center-technologies-are-force-multipliers/.

Frank, A. U. (1993). The use of geographical information systems: The user interface is the system. In D. Medyckyj-Scott & H. M. Hearnshaw (Eds.), *Human factors in geographic information systems* (pp. 3–14). London: Belhaven Press.

Frank, A., & Mark, D. (1991). Language issues for GIS. In D. Maguire, M. Goodchild, & D. Rhind (Eds.), *Geographic information systems: Principles* (pp. 147–163). Longman, London: Wiley.

Freundschuh, S. & Egenhofer, M. (1997). Human conceptions of spaces: Implications for geographic information systems. *Transactions in GIS, 2*(4), 361–375.

Fuhrmann, S., Huynh, N.T., & Scholz, R. (2013). Comparing fear of crime and crime statistics on a university campus. In *Crime Modeling and Mapping Using Geospatial Technologies* (pp. 319–337). Netherlands: Springer.

Garnier, S., Gautrais, J., & Theraulaz, G. (2007). The biological principles of swarm intelligence. *Swarm Intelligence, 1*, 3–31.

Gaziarifoglu, Y., Kennedy, L.W., & Caplan, J.M. (2012). Robbery risk as a co-function of place and time. Newark, NJ: Rutgers Center on Public Security. Retrieved from http://rutgerscps.weebly.com/uploads/2/7/3/7/27370595/robberyrtmtime_brief.pdf.

Gerber, M. (2014). Predicting crime using twitter and kernel density estimation. *Decision Support Systems, 61*, 115–125.

Glueck, S., & Glueck, E. (1950). *Unraveling juvenile delinquence.* New York: Commonwealth.

Golledge, R.G., & Stimson, R.J. (1997). *Spatial behavior: A geographic perspective.* New York, NY: Guildford Press.

Gorr, W., & Olligschlaeger, A. (2002). Crime hot spot forecasting: Modeling and comparative evaluation, final project report. NCJ 195167, Washington, DC: United States Department of Justice, National Institute of Justice.

Grassé, P. P. (1959). La reconstruction du nid et les coordinations inter-individuelles chez. *Bellicositermes Natalensis et Cubitermes* sp. La théorie de la stigmergie: Essai d'interprétation du comportement des termites constructeurs. *Insectes Sociaux, 6*, 41–81.

Groff, E.R., & La Vigne, N.G. (2002). Forecasting the future of predictive crime mapping. *Crime Prevention Studies, 13*, 29–58.

Groff, E.R., Weisburd, D., & Yang, S.M. (2010). Is it important to examine crime trends at a local "micro" level? A longitudinal analysis of block to block variability in crime trajectories. *Journal of Quantitative Criminology, 26*, 7–32.

Grubesic, T.H., & Mack, E.A. (2008). Spatio-temporal interaction of urban crime. *Journal of Quantitative Criminology, 24*(3), 285–306.

Guerette, R.T., & Bowers, K.J. (2009). Assessing the extent of crime displacement and diffusion of benefits: A review of situational crime prevention evaluations. *Criminology, 47*, 1331–1368.

Harries, K. (1999). *Mapping crime: Principles and practice.* Beverly Hills, CA: National Institute of Justice.

Hart, T.C., & Miethe, T.D. (2015). Configural behavior settings of crime event locations: Toward an alternative conceptualization of criminogenic microenvironments. *Journal of Research in Crime and Delinquency.* Advance online publication. doi:10.1177/0022427814566639.

Hart, T.C., & Zandbergen, P.A. (2012). *Effects of data quality on predictive hotspot mapping.* Washington, DC: National Institute of Justice.

Hart, T.C., & Zandbergen, P.A. (2013). Reference data and geocoding quality: Examining completeness and positional accuracy of street geocoded crime incidents. *Policing: An International Journal of Police Strategies and Management, 36*(2), 263–294.

Hatt, P. (1946). The concept of natural area. *American Sociological Review, 11*(4), 423–427.

Heffner, J. (2013). *Statistics of the RTMDx utility.* In J. Caplan, L. Kennedy, & E. Piza, *Risk terrain modeling diagnostics utility user manual (version 1.0).* Newark, NJ: Rutgers Center on Public Security.

Heitgerd, J. L., & Bursik, R. J. (1987). Extracommunity dynamics and the ecology of delinquency. *American Journal of Sociology, 92*(4), 775–787.

Henwood, K., Pidgeon, N., Parkhill, K., & Simmons, P. (2010). Researching risk: Narrative, biography, subjectivity. *Forum: Qualitative Social Research, 11*(1). Retrieved from http://www.qualitative-research.net/index.php/fqs/article/view/1438/2925.

Henwood, K. L., Pidgeon, N. F., Sarre, S., Simmons, P., & Smith, N. (2008). Risk, framing and everyday life: Methodological and ethical reflections from three sociocultural projects. *Health, Risk and Society, 10*, 421–438.

Hites, L. S., Fifolt, M., Beck, H., Su, W., Kerbawy, S., Wakelee, J., & Nassel, A. (2013). A geospatial mixed methods approach to assessing campus safety. *Evaluation Review, 35*(7), 347–369.

Hunter, R., & Jeffery, C. (1997). Preventing convenience store robbery through environmental design. In. R. Clarke (Ed.), *Situational Crime Prevention, successful case studies* (2nd ed.). Criminal Justice Press: Monsey, NY.

Infogroup. (2010). *Enhanced business and residential data: The importance of coverage, accuracy and recency for GIS data sets.* Infogroup: Government Division.

International Association for Chiefs of Police (IACP). (2003). Foot pursuits: Concepts and issues paper, 2003. Retrieved from http://www.tacp.org/getdoc/b69a2eb9-1ebd-4313-83fd-c5cd68825fff1/Foot_Pursuit_Paper.

International Association for Chiefs of Police (IACP). (2011). Law enforcement officers killed by felonious assault. Retrieved from www.theiacp.org/portals/o/pdfs/feloniousreport.pdf.

Irvin-Erickson, Y. (2014). Identifying risky places for crime: An analysis of the criminogenic spatiotemporal influences of landscape features on street robberies. (Unpublished doctoral dissertation). Rutgers University, Newark, NJ.

Jacobs, J. (1961/1992). *The death and life of great American cities.* New York: Random House.

Janson, C. G. (1980). Factorial social ecology: An attempt at summary and evaluation. *Annual Review of Sociology, 6*, 433–456.

Johnson, R. R. (2008). Officer firearms assaults at domestic violence calls: A descriptive analysis. *Police Journal, 81*(1), 25–45.

Johnson, S. D. (2008). Repeat burglary victimization: A tale of two theories. *Journal of Experimental Criminology, 4*, 215–240.

Johnson, S. D., Bernasco, W., Bowers, K. J., Elffers, H., Ratcliffe, J., Rengert, G., & Townsley, M. (2007). Space–time patterns of risk: A cross national assessment of residential burglary victimization. *Journal of Quantitative Criminology, 23*(3), 201–219.

Johnson, S. D., Bowers, K. J., Birks, D. J., & Pease, K. (2008). Prospective mapping: The importance of the environmental backcloth. In D. Weisburd, W. Bernasco, & G. Bruinsma (Eds.), *Putting crime in its place: Units of analysis in geographic criminology* (pp. 171–198). New York, NY: Springer.

Kaminski, R. J. (2007). Police foot pursuits and officer safety. *Law Enforcement Executive Forum, 7*(3), 59–72.

Kaminski, R. J., Jefferis, E., & Gu, J. (2003). Community correlates of serious assaults on police. *Police Quarterly, 6*, 119–149.

Kaminski, R. J., Rojek, J., Smith, H. P., & Alpert, G. P. (2012). Correlates of foot pursuit injuries in the Los Angeles County Sheriff's Department. *Police Quarterly, 15*(2), 177–196.

Kaminski, R. J., & Sorensen, D. W. (1995). A multivariate analysis of individual, situational and environmental factors associated with police assault injuries. *American Journal of Police*, 14(3–4), 3–48.

Kennedy, L. W. (1983). *The urban kaleidoscope: Canadian perspectives*. Toronto: McGraw-Hill Ryerson.

Kennedy, L. W., & Caplan, J. M. (2014). A theory of risky places (Research brief). Newark, NJ: Rutgers Center on Public Security.

Kennedy, L. W., Caplan, J. M., & Piza, E. (2011). Risk clusters, hotspots, and spatial intelligence: Risk terrain modeling as an algorithm for police resource allocation strategies. *Journal of Quantitative Criminology*, 27(3), 339–362.

Kennedy, L. W., Caplan, J. M., Piza, E. L. & Buccine-Schraeder, H. (2015, online first). Vulnerability and exposure to crime: Applying risk terrain modeling to the study of assault in Chicago. *Applied Spatial Analysis and Policy*.

Kennedy, L. W., & Forde, D. R. (1998). *When push comes to shove: A routine conflict approach to violence*. Albany, NY: State University of New York Press.

Kennedy, L. W., & Van Brunschot, E. G. (2009). *The risk in crime*. Lanham, MD: Rowman and Littlefield.

Kercher, C., Swedler, D. I., Pollack, K. M., & Webster, D. W. (2013). Homicides of law enforcement officers responding to domestic disturbance calls. *Injury Prevention*, 19(5), 331–335.

Kinney, J. B. (2010). Future spaces: Classics in environmental criminology—where do we go from here. In M. A. Andresen, P. J. Brantingham, & J. B. Kinney (Eds.), *Classics in environmental criminology* (pp. 481–487). Boca Raton, FL: CRC Press/Taylor & Francis.

Kinney, J. B., Brantingham, P. L., Wuschke, K., Kirk, M. G., & Brantingham, P. J. (2008). Crime attractors, generators and detractors: Land use and urban crime opportunities. *Built Environment*, 34(1), 62–74.

Koper, C. (1995). Just enough police presence: Reducing crime and disorderly behavior by optimizing patrol crime in crime hot spots. *Justice Quarterly*, 12(4), 649–672.

Koss. K. K. (2015). Leveraging predictive policing algorithms to restore Fourth Amendment protections in high-crime areas in post-Wardlow world. *Chicago-Kent Law Review*, 90(1), 300–334.

Lane, J., Gover, A. R., & Dahod, S. (2009). Fear of violent crime among men and women on campus: The impact of perceived risk and fear of sexual assault. *Violence and Victims*, 24(2), 172–192.

Langton M., & Durose L. (2011). Police behavior during traffic and street stops. Washington, DC: United States Department of Justice Office of Justice Programs, Bureau of Justice Statistics. Retrieved from http://www.bjs.gov/index.cfm?ty = pbdetail&iid = 4779.

Lee, M., & Alshalan, A. (2005). Geographic variation in property crime rates: A test of opportunity theory. *Journal of Crime and Justice*, 28(2), 101–127.

Lemieux, A., & Felson, M. (2012). Risk of violent crime victimization during major daily activities. *Violence and Victims*, 27(5), 635–655.

Louiselli, J. K., & Cameron, M. J. (Eds.). (1998). *Antecedent control: Innovative approaches to behavioral support*. Baltimore, MD: Brookes.

Loukaitou-Sideris, A. (1999). Hotspots of bus stop crime: The importance of environmental attributes. *Journal of American Planning Association*, 65(4), 395–411.

Lum, C. (2009). Translating police research into practice. Retrieved from http://www.policefoundation.org/sites/g/files/g798246/f/Ideas_Lum_0.pdf.

Lum, C., & Koper, C. S. (2013) Evidence-based policing in smaller agencies: Challenges, prospects, and opportunities. *Police Chief, 80*, 42–47.

Madensen, T. D., & Eck, J. E. (2008). *Spectator violence in stadiums.* Washington, DC: Office of Community Oriented Policing Services, US Department of Justice.

Maguire, K. (Ed.). (2007). Sourcebook of criminal justice statistics. Retrieved from http://www.albany.edu/sourcebook/pdf/t5452004.pdf.

Mark, D. (1993). Human spatial cognition. In D. Medyckyj-Scott & H. M. Hearnshaw (Eds.), *Human factors in geographical information systems* (pp. 51–60). London: Belhaven Press.

Mastrofski, S. D., Weisburd, D., & Braga, A. A. (2010). Rethinking policing: The policy implications of hotspots of crime. In N. A. Frost, J. D. Freilich, & T. R. Clear (Eds.), *Contemporary issues in criminal justice policy: Policy proposals from the American Society of Criminology conference* (pp. 251–264). Belmont, CA: Wadsworth.

Mazerolle, L., Kadleck, C., & Roehl, J. (1998). Controlling drug and disorder problems: The role of place managers. *Criminology, 36*(2), 371–402.

McGloin, J., Sullivan, C., & Kennedy, L. W. (Eds.). (2011). *When crime appears: The role of emergence.* New York, NY: Routledge.

McHarg, I. (1995). *Design with nature.* New York, NY: Wiley.

Mears, D. P., Scott, M. L., & Bhati, A. S. (2007). Opportunity theory and agricultural crime victimization. *Rural Sociology, 72*(2), 151–184.

Meyer, S., & Carroll R. H. (2013). When officers die: Understanding deadly domestic violence calls for service. *Police Chief.* Retrieved from http://www.policechiefmagazine.org/magazine/index.cfm?fuseaction = display_arch&article_id = 2378&issue_id = 52011.

Miethe, T. D., Stafford, M. C., & Long, J. S. (1987). Social differentiation in criminal victimization: A test of routine activities/lifestyle theories. *American Sociological Review, 52*(2), 184–194.

Miller, J., & Lin, J. (2007). Applying a generic juvenile risk assessment instrument to a local context: Some practical and theoretical lessons. *Crime and Delinquency, 53*, 552–580.

Montello, D. R. (1993). Scale and multiple psychologies of space. In A. U. Frank & I. Campari (Eds.), *Spatial information theory: A theoretical basis for GIS* (pp. 312–321). Berlin: Springer-Verlag.

Morenoff, J. D., Sampson R. J., & Raudenbush, S. W. (2001). Neighborhood inequality, collective efficacy, and the spatial dynamics of urban violence. *Criminology, 39*(3), 517–558.

Moreto, W. D., Piza, E., & Caplan, J. M. (2014). "A plague on both your houses?": Risks, repeats and reconsiderations of urban residential burglary. *Justice Quarterly, 31*(6), 1102–1126.

Murdie, R. (1969). Factorial Ecology of Metropolitan Toronto 1951–1961. Research paper no. 116, Department of Geography, University of Chicago.

National Highway Traffic Safety Administration (NHTSA). (2011). Characteristics of law enforcement officers' fatalities in motor vehicle crashes. Washington, DC: United States Department of Transportation, National Highway Traffic Safety Administration. Retrieved from http://www-nrd.nhtsa.dot.gov/Pubs/811411.pdf.

Newman, O. (1972). *Defensible space.* New York, NY: MacMillan.

Osgood, D. W., Wilson, J. K., O'Malley, P. M., Bachman, J. G., & Johnston, L. D. (1996). Routine activities and individual deviant behavior. *American Sociological Review, 61*(4), 635–655.

Park, R. E., McKenzie, R. D., & Burgess, E. (1925). *The city: Suggestions for the study of human nature in the urban environment.* Chicago, IL: University of Chicago Press.

Perry, W. L., McInnis, B., Price, C. C., Smith, S., & Hollywood, J. S. (2013). Predictive policing: The role of crime forecasting in law enforcement operations. Washington, DC: RAND Corporation. Retrieved from http://www.rand.org/content/dam/rand/pubs/research_reports/RR200/RR233/RAND_RR233.pdf.

Piza, E. L. (2012). Using Poisson and negative binomial regression models to measure the influence of risk on crime incident counts. Newark, NJ: Rutgers Center on Public Security. Retrieved from http://rutgerscps.weebly.com/uploads/2/7/3/7/27370595/countregressionmodels.pdf.

Quetelet, A. (1984). Research on the propensity for crime at different ages. (S. F. Sylvester, Trans.). Cincinnati, OH: Anderson. (Original work published 1831.)

Rabe-Hemp, C. E., & Schuck, A. M. (2007). Violence against police officers are female officers at greater risk? *Police Quarterly, 10*(4), 411–428.

Ratcliffe, J. (2006). A temporal constraint theory to explain opportunity-based spatial offending patterns. *Journal of Research in Crime and Delinquency, 43*(3), 261–291.

Ratcliffe, J. (2009). Near repeat calculator (version 1.3). Temple University, Philadelphia, PA; National Institute of Justice, Washington, DC. Retrieved from http://www.temple.edu/cj/misc/nr/.

Ratcliffe, J. (2010). The spatial dependency of crime increase dispersion. *Security Journal, 23*(1), 18–36.

Ratcliffe, J. H., & McCullagh, M. J. (1998). Identifying repeat victimization with GIS. *British Journal of Criminology, 38*(4), 651–662.

Ratcliffe, J. & Rengert, G. (2008). Near repeat patterns in Philadelphia shootings. *Security Journal, 21(1–2):* 58–76.

Ratcliffe, J., Taniguchi, T., Groff, E. R., & Wood, J. (2011). The Philadelphia foot patrol experiment: A randomized controlled trial of police effectiveness in violent crime hotspots. *Criminology, 49*(3), 795–831.

Reboussin, R., Warren, J., & Hazelwood, R. (1995). Mapless mapping in analyzing the spatial distribution of serial rapes. In C. Block, M. Dabdoub, & S. Fregley (Eds.), *Crime analysis through computer mapping* (pp. 69–74). Washington, DC: Police Executive Research Forum.

Rengert, G., & Lockwood, B. (2009). Geographical units of analysis and the analysis of crime. In D. Weisburd, W. Bernasco, & G. Bruinsma (Eds.), *Putting crime in its place: Units of analysis in geographic criminology.* New York: Springer.

Rengert, G., Ratcliffe, J. H., & Chakravorty, S. (2005). *Policing illegal drug markets: Geographic approaches to crime reduction.* Monsey, NY: Criminal Justice Press.

Roman, C. G. (2005). Routine activities of youth and neighborhood violence: Spatial modeling of place, time, and crime. In F. Wang (Ed.), *Geographic information systems and crime analysis* (pp. 293–310). Hershey, PA: Idea Group.

Roncek, D. (2000). Schools and crime. In V. Goldsmith, P. McGuire, J. Mollenkopf, & T. Ross (Eds.), *Analyzing crime patterns: Frontiers of practice* (pp. 153–167). Thousand Oaks, CA: Sage.

Roncek, D. W., Bell, R., & Francik, J. M. A. (1981). Housing projects and crime: Testing a proximity hypothesis. *Social Problems, 29*(2), 151–166.

Roncek, D. W., & Faggiani, D. (1985). High schools and crime: A replication. *Sociological Quarterly, 26*(4), 491–505.

Roncek, D. W., & Maier, P. A. (1991). Bars, blocks and crimes revisited: Linking the theory of routine activities to the empiricism of "hot spots." *Criminology, 29*(4), 725–753.

Sacco, V. & Kennedy, L. W. (2002). *The criminal event: Perspectives in space and time.* Belmont, CA: Wadsworth.

Scott, M. S., & Dedel, K. (2006). Assaults in and around bars (2nd ed.). United States Department of Justice: Office of Community Oriented Policing (COPS). Retrieved from http://www.popcenter.org/problems/assaultsinbars/print/.

Shane, J. M. (2012). Abandoned buildings and lots. In *Problem-Oriented Guides for Police.* Washington, DC: US Department of Justice, Office of Community Oriented Policing Services. Retrieved from http://www.popcenter.org/problems/abandoned_buildings_and_lots/.

Shaw, C., & McKay, H. (1969). *Juvenile delinquency and urban areas.* Chicago, IL: University of Chicago Press.

Sherman, L. (1995). Hotspots of crime and criminal careers of places. In J. E. Eck & D. Weisburd (Eds.), *Crime and Place, vol. 4* (pp. 35–52). Monsey, NY: Criminal Justice Press.

Sherman, L. W., Gartin, P. R., & Buerger, M. E. (1989). Hot spots of predatory crime: Routine activities and the criminology of place. *Criminology, 27*, 27–56.

Shevky, E., & Bell, W. (1955). Social area analysis. Stanford: Stanford University Press.

Short, M. B., Brantingham, P. J., Bertozzi, A. L., & Tita, G. E. (2010). Dissipation and displacement of hotspots in reaction-diffusion models of crime. *Proceedings of the National Academy of Sciences, 107*, 3961–3965.

Simon, R. (1975). *Women and crime.* Lexington, MA: Lexington Books.

Smit, S., van der Vecht, B., & Lebesque, L. (2014). Predictive mapping of anti-social behavior. *European Journal of Criminal Policy and Research.* Advance online publication. doi:10.1007/s10610-014-9259-1.

Snodgrass, J. (1976). Clifford R. Shaw and Henry D. McKay: Chicago criminologists. *British Journal Of Criminology, 16*(1), 1–19.

Sparrow, M. K. (2015). Measuring performance in a modern police organization. United States Department of Justice, National Institute of Justice.

Spelman, W. (1992). *Abandoned buildings: Magnets for crime?* Austin, TX: Lyndon Johnson School of Public Affairs (March). Photocopy.

Spiegel, A. (2015). *What heroin addiction tells us about changing bad habits.* Retrieved from http://www.npr.org/blogs/health/2015/01/05/371894919/what-heroin-addiction-tells-us-about-changing-bad-habits.

Stucky, T., & Ottensmann, J. (2009). Land use and violent crime. *Criminology, 47*(4), 1223–1264.

Taylor, B., Koper, C. S., & Woods, D. J. (2011). A randomized controlled trial of different policing strategies at hot spots of violent crime. *Journal of Experimental Criminology, 7*, 149–181.

Taylor, R.B. (1988). *Human territorial functioning*. New York, NY: University of Cambridge Press.

Taylor, R.B. (1997). Social order and disorder of street-blocks and neighborhood: Ecology, microecology and the systemic model of social disorganization. *Journal of Research in Crime and Delinquency, 24*, 113–155.

Taylor, R.B. & Harrell, A.V. (1996). *Physical environment and crime*. Washington, DC: National Institute of Justice.

Tiesman, H.M., Hendricks, S.A., Bell, J.L., & Amandus, H.A. (2010). Eleven years of occupational mortality in law enforcement: The census of fatal occupational injuries, 1992–2002. *American journal of industrial medicine, 53*(9), 940–949.

Tobler, W. (1970). A computer movie simulating urban growth in the Detroit region. *Economic Geography, 46*(2), 234–240.

Tomlin, C.D. (1991). "Cartographic Modeling." In D.J. Maguire, M.F. Goodchild, & D.W. Rhind (Eds.), *Geographical information systems: Principles and applications* (pp. 361–374). Harlow, UK: Longman.

Tomlin, C.D. (1994). Map algebra: One perspective. *Landscape and Urban Planning, 30*(1), 3–12.

Tseng, C.H., Duane, J., & Hadipriono, F. (2004). Performance of campus parking garages in preventing crime. *Journal of Performance of Constructed Facilities, 18*, 21–28.

Tucker-Gail, K.A., Selman, D., Kobolt, J.R., & Hill, T. (2010). Felonious line-of-duty officer deaths (1995–1999): The impact of tenure and age. *International Journal of Police Science & Management, 12*(1), 119–133.

Van Brunschot, E. & Kennedy, L.W. (2008). *Risk Balance and Security*. Thousand Oaks, CA: Sage.

Van Patten, I.T., McKeldin-Coner, J., & Cox, D. (2009). A microspatial analysis of robbery: Prospective hot spotting in a small city. *Crime Mapping, 1,* 7–32.

Walker, B.B., Schuurman, N., & Hameed, S.M. (2014). A GIS-based spatiotemporal analysis of violent trauma hotspots in Vancouver, Canada: Identification, contextualization and intervention. *BJM Open, 4*(2). Retrieved from http://www.ncbi.nlm.nih.gov/pmc/articles /PMC3931990/.

Weisburd, D. (2008). Place-based policing. *Ideas in policing series*. Washington, DC: Police Foundation.

Weisburd, D., & Braga, A.A. (2006). Hotspots policing as a model for police innovation. In D. Weisburd & A.A. Braga (Eds.), *Police innovation: Contrasting perspectives* (pp. 225–244). New York, NY: Cambridge University Press.

Weisburd, D., Groff, E., & Yang, S. (2012). *The criminology of place: Street segments and our understanding of the crime problem*. Oxford: Oxford University Press.

Weisburd, D., and Piquero, A.R. (2008). How well do criminologists explain crime? Statistical modeling in published studies. *Crime and Justice, 37*(1), 453–502.

Wells, W., Wu, L., & Ye, X. (2011). Patterns of near-repeat gun assaults in Houston. *Journal of Research in Crime and Delinquency, 49*(2), 186–212.

Wilcox, P., & Gialopsos, B.M. (2015). Crime event criminology: An overview. *Journal of Contemporary Criminal Justice, 31*(1), 4–11.

Wortley, R. (2001). A classification of techniques for controlling situational precipitators of crime. *Security Journal, 14*(4), 63–82.

Wortley, R. (2002). *Situational prison control: Crime prevention in correctional institutions.* Cambridge: Cambridge University Press.

Wortley, R. (2008). Situational crime precipitators. In R. Wortley (Ed.), *Environmental criminology and crime analysis* (pp. 48–69). Evanston, IL: Willan.

Yerxa, M. (2013). Evaluating the temporal parameters of risk terrain modeling with residential burglary. *Crime Mapping, 5*(1), 7–38.

Zahm, D. (2007). Crime prevention through environmental design in problem-solving. United States Department of Justice: Office of Community Oriented Policing (COPS). Retrieved from http://www.popcenter.org/tools/pdfs/cpted.pdf.

INDEX